# CONSIDER THE SOURCE: DOCUMENTS IN LATIN AMERICAN HISTORY

### Julie A. Charlip
*Whitman College*

# LATIN AMERICA:
## AN INTERPRETIVE HISTORY

### EIGHTH EDITION

### E. Bradford Burns
*University of California, Los Angeles*

### Julie A. Charlip
*Whitman College*

PEARSON

Prentice
Hall

Upper Saddle River, New Jersey 07458

© 2007 by PEARSON EDUCATION, INC.
Upper Saddle River, New Jersey 07458

10 9 8 7 6 5 4 3 2 1

ISBN 0-13-194144-5

Printed in the United States of America

# Table of Contents

# Introduction

Imagine this scene: You sit down to lunch with your roommate, who shares with you a juicy bit of gossip about someone in your dorm. Knowing the person in question, you find the story a bit hard to believe. "Who told you that?" you ask. It turns out that the story originates with a mutual acquaintance, someone who in the past has been found to be less than trustworthy. You snort derisively and say, "Well, consider the source." Indeed.

Historians rely on a variety of sources–written, visual, oral, material–to find out what happened in the past and analyze why things unfolded in the way that they did. Sources from the time period being studied are referred to as primary sources. Secondary sources are the history books, or monographs, written from those sources, the kind of books in the "recommended reading" lists at the end of each chapter in the textbook.

Primary sources include government documents, speeches, diaries, letters and newspapers, which tend to reflect official and elite views of what occurred. Getting to the source of popular voices is more challenging, but it be done through such things as folk tales and proverbs, popular songs, test in police and court records, and interviews (oral histories) with participa Statistics are a great source of general patterns in society.

Fiction can also be a rich source if used carefully. As an hi clear of so-called historical novels that aim to put words in the m figures; they may be entertaining, but can be historically misle novels written in a particular time reflect the concerns and at While the characters are fictional, their views and situatior historic reality.

1

Keep in mind, however, that there are multiple realities, reflecting the positions of different participants. Viewpoints are affected by material conditions, political and social relationships, religion, ethnicity, race, class and gender. And that is equally true for the viewpoints of the historians, who choose their subjects and questions based on who they are and the ways in which they see reality.

There is no such thing as objectivity, an indisputable truth on which all can agree. At least, none of the truly interesting elements of history are objective. Perhaps everyone can agree that a long and bloody war began in Mexico in 1910. But what kind of war was it? A revolution? A civil war? A peasant war? A bourgeois struggle? And who really won? It is in the analysis that history really becomes interesting.

All of these sources are subject to interpretation and should not be taken at face value. You need to consider the source: Who is writing? What biases might the source reflect?

With all their limitations, the primary sources are all that we have to piece together history. The sources do speak, although not always as loudly and clearly as historians might like. Listen carefully to their voices.

# EVALUATING A DOCUMENT

## The Time and Place Rule

In making initial judgments about the quality of a primary source, the historians' first rule of thumb is that the closer in time and place the source (and its creator) was to an event in the past, the better the source. In order of priority, sources might run as follows:

- Direct traces of the event.
- Descriptions of the event written at the time of the event by firsthand observers and participants.
- Accounts of the event written (or otherwise created) by people who participated or witnessed it firsthand, but written after the event occurred.
- Accounts of the event written by people who did not participate or witness the event, but who use then-contemporary information.

## The Bias Rule

The historians' second rule of thumb is that every source is biased in some way. No document can tell us more than what the author of the document thought had happened or perhaps only what the author wanted others to think had happened. As a result:

- Every individual piece of evidence and every source must be read or viewed skeptically and critically.
- No piece of evidence should be taken at face value.
- Each piece of evidence and source must be cross-checked or compared with other related sources and pieces of evidence.

Source: American Memory, Library of Congress
http://www.cms.ccsd.k12.co.us/ss/SONY/psbeta2/pshome.htm#student

# WORKSHEET FOR ANALYZING PRIMARY SOURCES

Identify the Source

What type of document is it?

General categories include contemporary history, public documents generated by branches of government; such as laws, decrees, reports, speeches, budgets, civil registries, census data, police and court records; church records; private business accounts; private letters, diaries, and journals; newspaper and magazine articles, editorials and advertising; literary sources such as novels, poetry and short stories; popular folk tales, jokes and songs; photography, artwork, and objects.

Where is the document from?

When was it written?

Who wrote it?

Analyze the Source

What does the document talk about?
What does it not talk about? (To answer this question, you need to draw on your knowledge from secondary sources and compare this document with other primary sources.)
Why was it written? What is the document's purpose? (Consider what motivated the author and how that motivation might affect what information is presented and the manner in which it is presented.)
Who was the document written for? (Consider that documents written for different audiences might provide different information.)
What kinds of questions can be answered with this source?
What questions cannot be answered using this document?
What makes this particular source valuable?

Make note of

People mentioned in the document.
Words and phrases that might have a special or different meaning.
Allusions to events.
Assumptions made by the author.

# CHAPTER 1: LAND AND PEOPLE

Latin America's physical attributes struck both newcomer and inhabitants alike. Here four observers comment on its wonders. First, Christopher Columbus writes to Lord Raphael Sanchez, treasurer to "their most invincible Majesties, Ferdinand and Isabella," during his first voyage in 1492, describing the island of Cuba, which he named Juana, and Hispaniola, the island that today comprises Haiti and the Dominican Republic. Then, the physician for Columbus' fleet, Dr. Chanca, writes to the Chapter of Seville during the second voyage in 1493, further describing the Caribbean Islands. Both accounts are taken from a reprint of the original letters of Columbus, published in 1847 and translated and edited by R. H. Major. Columbus's letter was originally in Latin, Chanca's in Spanish. Next, Prussian botanist Alexander Von Humboldt writes of his travels in the Spanish Colonies (1799-1804) in his self-published *Personal Narrative of Travels to the Equinoctial Regions of America,* published in multiple volumes from 1808-1827. Finally, Gabriela Mistral writes "My Homeland," an ode to Chile published in a 1923 newspaper. In 1945 Mistral became the first Latin American to win the Nobel Prize for literature.

# First Voyage of Columbus

This said island of Juana is exceedingly fertile, as indeed are all the others; it is surrounded with many bays, spacious very secure, and surpassing any that I have ever seen; numerous large and healthful rivers intersect it, and it also contains many very lofty mountains. All these islands are very beautiful, and distinguished by a diversity of scenery; they are filled with a great variety of trees of immense height, and which I believe to retain their foliage in all seasons; for when I saw them they were as verdant and luxuriant as they usually are in Spain in the month of May—and some of them were blossoming, some bearing fruit, and all flourishing in the greatest perfection, according to their respective stages of growth, and the nature and quality of each—yet the islands are not so thickly wooded as to be impassable. The nightingale and various birds were singing in countless numbers, and that in November, the month in which I arrived there. There are besides in the same island of Juana seven or eight kinds of palm trees, which, like all the other trees, herbs, and fruits, considerably surpass ours in height and beauty. The pines also are very handsome, and there are very extensive fields and meadows, a variety of birds, different kinds of honey, and many sorts of metals, but no iron. In that island also which I have before said we named Española, there are mountains of very great size and beauty, vast plains, groves, and very fruitful fields, admirably adapted for tillage, pasture, and habitation. The convenience and excellence of the harbours in this island, and the abundance of the rivers, so indispensable to the health of man, surpass anything that would be believed by one who had not seen it. The trees, herbage, and fruits of Española are very different from those of Juana, and moreover it abounds in various kinds of spices, gold, and other metals.

Source:  Christopher Columbus, *Four voyages to the New World: letters and selected documents*. Translated and edited by R.H. Major. N.Y.: Carol Publishing Group, 1992, 4-5.

# Second Voyage of Columbus

[T]here were six islands to be seen lying in different directions, and most of them of considerable size. We directed our course towards that which we had first seen,[1] and reaching the coast, we proceeded more than a league in search of a port where we might anchor, but without finding one: all that part of the island which we could observe, appeared mountainous, very beautiful, and green even up to the water, which was delightful to see, for at that season, there is scarcely anything green in our own country. [T]he Admiral decided that we should go to the other island[2]. This island was filled with an astonishingly thick growth of wood; the variety of unknown trees, some bearing fruit and some flowers, was surprising, and indeed every spot was covered with verdure. We found there a tree whose leaf had the finest smell of cloves that I have ever met with; it was like a laurel leaf, but not so large; but I think it was a species of Laurel.

There were wild fruits of various kinds, some of which our men, not very prudently, tasted; and upon only touching them with their tongues, their countenances became inflamed,[3] and such great heat and pain followed, that they seemed to be made, and were obliged to resort to refrigerants to cure themselves. [O]n the following morning we left for another very large island[4]. We approached it under the side of a great mountain, that seemed almost to reach the skies, in the middle of which rose a peak, higher than all the rest of the mountain, whence many streams diverged into different channels. At three

---

[1] The island of Dominica.

[2] The island of Marigalante, named for the ship in which they traveled.

[3] Identified as manzanillo in 1847 by Martín Fernández de Navarrette, Director of the Royal Academy of History of Madrid.

[4] The island of Guadaloupe.

8

leagues distance, we could see an immense fall of water, which discharged itself from such a height that it appeared to fall from the sky; it was seen from so great a distance that it occasioned many wagers to be laid on board the ships, some maintaining that it was but a series of white rocks, and others that it was water. When we came nearer to it, it showed itself distinctly, and it was the most beautiful thing in the world to see from how great a height and from what a small space so large a fall of water was discharged. When we reached Española the land, at the part where we approached it was low and very flat. The country is very remarkable, and contains a vast number of large rivers, and extensive chains of mountains, with broad, open valleys, and the mountains are very high; it does not appear that the grass is ever cut throughout the year. I do not think they have any winter in this part, for near Navidad (at Christmas) were found many birds-nests, some containing the young birds, and other containing eggs. No four-footed animal has ever been seen in this or any of the other islands, except some dogs of various colours, as in our own country, but in shape like large house-dogs; and also some little animals, in colour, size, and fur, like a rabbit, with long tails, and feet like those of a rat; these animals climb up the trees, and many who have tasted them, say they are very good to eat;[5] there are not any wild beasts. There are great numbers of small snakes, and some lizards, but not many; for the Indians consider them as great a luxury as we do pheasants; they are of the same size as ours, but different in shape. In a small adjacent island[6] (in which is a port called Monte Christo, where we stayed several days), our men saw an enormous kind of lizard, which they said was as

---

[5] Likely a species of capromys, a rodent generally known in Cuba as an hutia.
[6] Isla Cabritos, located within Lake Enriquillo in Hispaniola.

large round as a calf, with a tail as long as a lance, which they often went out to kill; but bulky as it was, it got into the sea, so that they could not catch it.

Source: Christopher Columbus, *Four voyages to the New World: letters and selected documents.* Translated and edited by R.H. Major. N.Y.: Carol Publishing Group, 1992, 21-24, 39-41.

# Alexander von Humboldt Travels in South America

On the third and fourth of July we crossed that part of the Atlantic Ocean where charts indicate the Maelstrom; at night we changed course to avoid the danger, though its existence is— dubious. The old charts are filled with rocks, some of which really exist, though most are due to optical illusions, which are more frequent at sea than on land.

From the time we entered the torrid zone we never tired of admiring, night after night, the beauty of the southern sky, which as we advanced further south opened up new constellations.
A strange, completely unknown feeling is awoken in us when nearing the equator and crossing from one hemisphere to another; the stars we have known since infancy begin to vanish. Nothing strikes the traveler more completely about the immense distances that separate him from home than the look of a new sky, everything on earth and in the sky in the tropical countries takes an exotic note.

When a traveler recently arrived from Europe steps into A South American jungle for the first time he sees nature in a completely unexpected guise. The objects that surround him only faintly bring to mind those descriptions by famous writers of the banks of the Mississippi, of Florida and of other temperate regions of the New World. With each step he feels not at the frontiers of the torrid zone but in its midst; not on one of the West Indian Islands but in a vast continent where everything is gigantic; mountains, rivers and the masses of plants. If he is able to feel the beauty of the landscape, he will find it hard to analyze his many impressions. He does not know what shocks him more; whether the calm silence of the solitude, or the beauty of the diverse, contrasting objects, or that fullness and freshness of plant life in the Tropics. It could be said that the earth, overloaded with plants, does not have sufficient space to develop. Everywhere tree trunks are hidden behind a thick green carpet. If you carefully transplanted all the orchids, all the ephiphytes that grown on one single American fig tree (*Ficus gigantea*) you would manage to cover an enormous amount of ground. The same lianas that trail along the ground climb up to the tree-tops, swinging from one tree to another hundred feet up in the air. As these parasitical plants form a real tangle, a botanist often confuses flowers, fruit and leaves belonging to different species.

We walked for hours in the shade of these plant vaults that scarcely let us catch glimpses of the blue sky, which appeared to be more of a deep indigo blue because the green, verging on brown, of tropical plants seemed so intense. A great fern tree (perhaps *Aspidium caducum*) rose above masses of scattered rock. For the first time we saw those nests in the shape of bottles or small bags that hang from the lower branches. They are the work of that clever builder the Oriole, whose song blends with the noisy shrieking of Parrots and Macaws. These last, so well– known for their vivid colours, fly around in pairs, while the parrots proper fly in flocks of hundreds. A man must live in these regions, particularly the hot Andean valleys, to understand how these birds can sometimes drown the noise of waterfalls with their voices.

Days passed quickly in the Capuchin convent in the Caripe mountains, despite our simple but monotonous life. From sunrise to sunset, we toured the forests and mountains nearby.

This site has something wild and tranquil, melancholic and attractive about it. In the midst of such powerful nature we felt nothing inside but peace

12

and repose. In the solitude of these mountains I was less struck by the new impressions recorded at each step than by the fact that such diverse climates have so much in common. In the hills where the convent stands, palm trees and tree fern grow. In the afternoon, before the rainfalls, the monotonous screaming of the howler monkeys seems like a distant wind in the forests. Despite these exotic sounds, and the strange plant forms and marvels of the New World, everywhere nature allows man to sense a voice speaking to him in familiar terms. The grass carpeting the sound, the old moss and ferns covering tree roots, the torrent that falls over steep calcareous rocks, the harmonious colours reflecting the water, the green and the sky, all evoke familiar sensations in the traveler.

Source: Alexander von Humboldt, *Personal narrative of a Journey to the Equinoctial Regions of the New Continent.* Abridged and translated by Jason Wilson. N.Y.: Penguin Books, 1995, 41-2, 83-4, 108-109.

# Gabriela Mistral, "My Homeland"

Chile: a land so small that it comes to look on the map like a beach between a mountain chain and a sea; a parenthesis between two dominant centurions and to the south the tragic caprice of the antarctic archipelago, torn into pieces, creating an immense laceration in the ocean's velvet.

And the natural zones, clear, defined, reflecting the character of the race. To the north, the desert, the salt bank, whitened by the sun, where man proves himself through effort and pain. Immediately thereafter, the transition zone, devoted to mining and agriculture, the provider of the race's most vigorous fellows: a landscape of austere sobriety, akin to an ardent spirituality. Then comes the agrarian zone, with its affable landscape, joyous spots from its fields and dense spots populated by factories; the placid shadow of a peasant rupturing itself through the valleys, and the working masses walking like agile ants in the cities. At the southern end the cold tropic, with a jungle that exhales in the same manner as the one in Brazil, but one that is black, dispossessed of the color's lechery; islands rich in fishing, wrapped in a livid mist, and the *Patagonian* plateau, horizontal and desolate, our only land blessed with a broad sky, a pastoral land for the innumerable cattle herding below the mountain snow.

Small land, not small nation. Reduced soil, inferior to the ambitions and the heroic nature of its people. It does not matter: we have the sea ... the sea ... the sea!


Source: *The Oxford Book of Latin American Essays*, Ed. Ilan Stavans. New York: Oxford University Press, 1997, 84-5.

# CHAPTER 2: FROM CONQUEST TO EMPIRE

The long relationship between Spain and the New World began with the

conquest. War was nothing new to the indigenous, but the nature and result of

warfare with Spain was quite different than the traditions of the indigenous.

Here are two visions of the conquest: Bernal Díaz del Castillo recounts his

exploits with Hernando Cortes (1519-21) in his memoirs, written mostly in the

1560s. A Nahua view is offered nobles who were trained by Franciscan priest

Bernardino de Sahagún to write in Nahuatl using the Latin alphabet. The texts,

known as the Florentine Codex, were written from 1545-76.

The institutions of empire were more important than the conquest for

maintaining three hundred years of colonial domination. Chief among the

institutions were labor arrangements, beginning with the *encomienda*, a grant of

the labor and tribute of indigenous workers to a Spanish *encomendero*. Queen

Isabella approved the institution, but not all Spaniards were so rewarded, as we

see in the words of Melchor Verdugo, Bartolomé Garcia, and doña Isabel

de Guevara.

The small number of Spaniards could not possibly have guaranteed the

labor and tribute of the indigenous without the help of traditional leaders. The

Spanish refashioned the old Indian councils of elders into Spanish-style *cabildos*

and used them to pass on their orders. The indigenous cabildo members quickly

learned to appeal to higher ups when local burdens seemed excessive. It is

unlikely, however, that anyone on the Council of the Indies read the documents,

like the one included here, which were written in Nahuatl.

Where there was the promise of a lucrative export product but

insufficient indigenous labor, the Spanish and Portuguese turned to Africa for slaves. Olaudah Equiano gives an account of the horror of being taken into captivity in Nigeria.

# A Conquistador's View

We proceeded along the causeway which is here eight paces in width and runs so straight to the City of Mexico that it does not seem to me to turn either much or little, but, broad as it is, it was so crowded with people that there was hardly room for them all, some of them going to and others returning from Mexico, besides those who had come to see us, so that we were hardly able to pass by the crowds of them that came; and the towers and cues were full of people as well as the canoes from all parts of the lake. It was not to be wondered at, for they had never before seen horses or men such as we are.

Gazing on such wonderful sights, we did not know what to say, or whether what appeared before us was real, for on one side, on the land, there were great cities, and in the lake ever so many more, and the lake itself was crowded with canoes, and in the Causeway were many bridges at intervals, and in front of us stood the great City of Mexico, and we—we did not even number four hundred soldiers! And we well remembered the words and warnings given us by the people of Huexotzingo and Tlaxcala, and the many other warnings that had been given that we should beware of entering Mexico, where they would kill us, as soon as they had us inside.

Let the curious readers consider whether there is not much to ponder over in this that I am writing. What men have there been in the world who have shown such daring?

We made attacks on the Mexicans every day and succeeded in capturing many idle towers, houses, canals, and other openings and bridges which they had constructed from house to house, and we filled them all up with adobes and the timbers from the houses that we pulled down and destroyed and

17

we kept guard over them, but notwithstanding all this trouble that we took, the enemy came back and deepened them and widened the openings and erected more barricades. And because our three companies considered it a dishonour that some should be fighting and facing the Mexican squadrons and other should be filling up passes and openings and bridges, Pedro de Alvarado, so as to avoid quarrels as to who should be fighting or filling up openings, ordered that one company should have charge of the filling in and look after that work one day, while the other two companies should fight and face the enemy, and that this should be done in rotation one day one company, and another day another company, until each company should have had its turn, and owing to this arrangement there was nothing captured that was not razed to the ground, and our friends the Tlaxcalans helped us. So we went on penetrating into the City.

Once more, as soon as another day dawned, all the greatest forces that Guatemoc could collect were already down upon us, and as we had filled up the opening and causeway and bridge, they could pass it dryshod. My faith! They had the daring to come up to our ranchos and hurl javelins and stones and arrows, but with the cannon we could always make them draw off, for Pedro Moreno, who had charge of the cannon, did much damage to the enemy. I wish to say that they shot our own arrows at us from crossbows, for while they held five crossbowmen alive, and Cristóbal de Guzman with them, they made them load the crossbows and show them how they were to be discharged, and either they or the Mexicans discharged those shots deliberately, but they did no harm with them.

18

Source: Bernal Diaz del Castillo, *The discovery and conquest of Mexico, 1517-1521*, edited from the only exact copy of the original MS (and published in Mexico) by Genaro García. Translated with an introduction and notes by A. P. Maudslay. Introduction to the American edition by Irving A. Leonard. New York: Farrar, Straus and Cudahy, 1956, 191-2, 422-23, 441.

# A Nahua View of Conquest

The Spaniards mounted a wooden catapult on the temple platform to fling stones as the Indians. While it was being set up, the Indians who had gathered in Amaxac came out to stare at it. They pointed at the machine and asked each other what it could be. When the Spaniards had finished their preparations and were ready to shoot it at the crowd, they wound it up until the wooden beams stood erect. Then they released it like a great sling.

But the stone did not fall among the Indians. It flew over their heads and crashed into a corner of the marketplace. This seemed to cause an argument among the Spaniards: they gestured toward the Indians and shouted at each other. But still they could not aim the machine correctly. It threw out its stones in every direction.

Finally the Indians were able to see how it worked: it had a sling inside it, worked by a heavy rope. The Indians named it "the wooden sling."

The Spaniards and Tlaxcaltecas retreated again.

Our warriors rallied to defend the city. Their spirits and courage were high; not one of them showed any fear or behaved like a woman. They cried: "Mexicanos, come here and join us! Who are these savages? A mere rabble from the south!" They did not move in a direct line; they moved in a zigzag course, never in a straight line.

The Spanish soldiers often disguised themselves so that they would not be recognized. They wore cloaks like those of the Aztecs and put on the same battle dress and adornments, hoping to deceive our warriors into thinking they were not Spaniards.

Whenever the Aztecs saw the enemy notching their arrows, they either dispersed or flattened themselves on the ground. The warriors of Tlatelolco were very alert; they were very cautious and vigilant, and watched intently to see where the shots were coming from.

But step by step the Spaniards gained more ground and captured more houses. They forced us backward along the Amaxac road with their spears and shields.

Once again the Spaniards started killing and a great many Indians died. The flight from the city began and with this the war came to an end. The people cried: "We have suffered enough! Let us leave the city! Let us go live on weeds!" Some fled across the lake, others along the causeways, and even then there were many killings. The Spaniards were angry because our warriors still carried their shields and *macanas*.[7]

Those who lived in the center of the city went straight toward Amaxac, to the fork in the road. From there they fled in various directions, some toward Tepeyacac, others toward Xoxohuiltitlan and Nonohualco; Those who lived in boats or on the wooden rafts anchored in the lake fled by the water, as did the inhabitants of Tolmyaecan. Some of them waded in water up to their chests and even up to their necks. Others drowned when they reached water above their heads.

The Spanish soldiers were stationed along the roads to search the fleeing inhabitants. They were looking only for gold and paid no attention to jade, turquoise or quetzal feathers. The women carried their gold under their skirts and the men carried it in their mouths or under their loincloths . . . but the

---

[7] A flattened club edged with sharpened pieces of obsidian.

Spaniards searched all the women without exception: those with light skins, those with dark skins, those with dark bodies.

Source: *The broken spears: the Aztec account of the conquest of Mexico,* Miguel León-Portilla, ed. translated from Nahuatl into Spanish by Angel María Garibay K.; English translation by Lysander Kemp (Boston: Beacon Press, 1992), 92-3, 111-112, 117-119.

# The Queen Approves Encomiendas

Medina del Campo, December 20, 1503, Isabella, by the Grace of God, Queen of Castile, etc. In as much as the King, my Lord, and I, in the instruction we commanded given to Don Fray Nicholas de Ovando, Comendador Mayor of Alcantara, at the time when he went to the islands and mainland of the Ocean Sea, decreed that the Indian inhabitants and residents of the island of Española, are free and not subject . . . and as now we are informed that because of the excessive liberty enjoyed by the said Indians that they will not even work for wages, but wander about idle, and cannot be had by the Christians to convert to the Holy Catholic Faith; and in order that the Christians of the said island . . . many not lack people to work their holdings for their maintenance, and may be able to take out what gold there is on the island . . . and because we desire that the said Indians be converted to our Holy Catholic Faith and taught in its doctrines; and because this can better be done by having the Indians living in community with the Christians of the island, and by having them go among them and associate with them, by which means they will help each other to cultivate and settle and increase the fruits of the island and take the gold which may be there and bring profit to my kingdom and subjects.

I have commanded this my letter to be issued on the matter, in which I command you, our said Governor, that beginning from the day you receive my letter you will compel and force the said Indians to associate with the Christians of the island and to work on their buildings, and to gather and mine the gold and other metals, and to till the fields and produce food for the Christian inhabitants and dwellers of the said island; and you are to have each one paid on the day he works the wage and maintenance which you think he should have—and you are

23

to order each cacique to take charge of a certain number of the said Indians so that you may make them work wherever necessary, and so that on feast days and such days as you think proper they may be gathered together to hear and be taught in matters of the Faith--this the Indians shall perform as free people, which they are, and not as slaves. And see to it that the said Indians are well treated, those who become Christians better than the others, and do not consent or allow that any person do them any harm or oppress them.

I, the Queen

Source:  E. Bradford Burns, *Latin America: Conflict and Creation, A Historical Reader* (Englewood Cliffs, N.J.: Prentice Hall, 1993), 36-37; citing Lesley Byrd Sympson, *The Encomienda in New Spain. The Beginning of Spanish Mexico*, 3rd ed. (Berkeley: University of California Press, 1956), 30-31.

# Spaniards and Encomiendas

Successful encomendero Melchor Verdugo writes to his mother, 1536:

Lady:

I live in a place called Trujillo [Peru] and have my house there and a very good encomiendas of Indians, with about eight or ten thousand vassals; I think there's never a year that they don't give me 5,000 or 6,000 pesos in income. I write you all this so you'll be glad and know that I live without necessity, praise our Lord.

With the bearer of the present letter I am sending to ask certain favors of his majesty, among which I'm sending to request a perpetual grant of my Indians for me and my heirs.

Your obedient son who kisses your hands, Melchor Verdugo.

The unsuccessful Bartolomé García writes to the Council of the Indies, 1556:

Very powerful lords:

As a man who has been wronged, I cannot refrain from complaining to your highness as my king.

At the end of twenty years the governor of this province [Paraguuay] gave its natives in encomiendas to those who are just newly arrived and to others who came after we did. Of those who conquered the land, some of them losing their sons and some their brothers, there remain, from the 1,700 men counted at the muster don Pedro de Mendoza held when he landed, about a hundred men, and to them the governor gave the worst grants and the most distant, from where one can get no service. And so, many have not wished to accept the grants, of whom I am one, since he gave me sixteen Indians eighty leagues from where we live, and he gave others fifteen, or twenty, or thirty, but for his sons-in-law, and sons-in-law of his sons-in-law, and the officials of your highness and for himself, he took the whole country, all the best part of it.

Your vassal who kisses your royal feet, Bartolomé García.

Doña Isabel de Guevara complains to the princess, doña Juana, 1556:

Very high and powerful lady:

Several women came to this province of the Río de la Plata along with its first governor don Pedro de Mendoza, and it was my fortune to be one of them. On reaching the port of Buenos Aires, our expedition contained 1,500 men, but food was scarce, and the hunger was such that within three months 1,000 of them died. The men became so weak that all the tasks fell on the poor women, washing the clothes as well as nursing the men, preparing them the little food there was, keeping them clean, standing guard, patrolling the fires, loading the crossbows when the Indians came sometimes to do battle, even firing the cannon, and arousing the soldiers who were capable of fighting, shouting the alarm through the camp, acting as sergeants and putting soldiers in order, because at that time, as we women can make do with little nourishment, we had not fallen into such weakness as the men. If it had not been for us, all would have perished; and were it not for the men's reputation, I could truthfully write you much more.

Afterwards they decided to ascend the Paraná in search of provisions, in which voyage the unfortunate women underwent such hardships that God gave them life miraculously because he saw that the men's lives depended on them, for they took all the tasks of the ship so to hear that a woman who did less than another felt affronted; they worked the sail, steered the ship, sounded the

26

depth, bailed out the water, took the oar when a soldier was unable to row, and exhorted the soldiers not to be discouraged, that men were meant for hardships. Thus they arrived at this city of Asunción, and the women had to turn to their tasks anew, making clearings with their own hands, clearing and hoeing and sowing and harvesting the crops with no one's aid until such time as the soldiers recovered from their weakness and began to rule the land.

I wanted to write this and bring it to your highness' attention to let you know how ungratefully I have been treated in this land.—I was left out without being given the service of a single Indian.—So I beg you to order that my encomiendas be granted to me in perpetuity, and that in gratification of my services my husband be appointed to some office suiting the quality of his person, since for his own part, his services merit it.

Your highness' servant who kisses your royal hands, Doña Isabel de Guevara

Source: *Letters and People of the Spanish Indies, Sixteenth Century,* translated and edited by James Lockhart and Enrique Otte. (Cambridge: Cambridge University Press, (c) 1976). Reprinted with permission of Cambridge University Press.

# An Indigenous Cabildo Writes to the Crown, 1554

Our much revered ruler:

We Mexica and Tenochca bow down to you and kiss your precious hands and feet, you our ruler and prince who guard over things for our lord Jesus Christ there in old Spain and here in New Spain; we set before you our weeping, tears, and great concern, for well we know that you greatly love us your poor vassals who are citizens here in New Spain, as it is called.

Your benevolence appears in the very good orders with which you and your precious father our great Emperor have defended us. If your orders for us had been carried out, we would have had no concern and would have lived in great happiness. We think that it is because of our failings that your orders have been fruitless, which greatly increases our concern, so that it is not for nothing that we put before you our weeping, tears and concerns.

Listen, our much revered ruler and prince; although you have sent many orders here to benefit us your poor vassals, those who serve you and exercise your rulership here in New Spain do not carry them out, which causes us great suffering and loss of possessions and property, now and in the past. And although it is very piteous and worrisome, we merely set our weeping and tears before our god and ruler God our Lord so that he will remedy it when he wishes.

There is another great affliction of ours which now newly concerns us, with which we cry out to you, our precious prince, for now in the year 1554 the rule and governorship that our fathers and grandfathers bequeathed us was going to be taken from us and given to the Spaniards. And, oh king, it would have been carried out if our fathers the Friars of San Francisco had not supported us;

they would have made us all their slaves. And those who wish to do this are making every effort to carry it out; we think that they will indeed impose their will on us if you and your precious father do not defend us. Two alcaldes mayores were appointed, one to serve in Mexico City and the other in Tlatelolco, and they were to be in charge of the governorship, justice and town council business. When we heard of the order we brought complaint before your representative don Luis de Velasco the viceroy, and the Friars of San Francisco also spoke to him on our behalf. Then he gave orders that the two should not be called alcaldes mayores but only protectors, and he instructed them that their only duty would be to save us from any Spaniard, mestizo, Black or mulatto molesting us in the marketplace, on the roads, in the canals, or in our homes; he instructed them to be on the watch day and night that no one molest us. We greatly approve this order of your viceroy, for we need it very much, and we implore you to order them to take great care with their task, for the Spaniards, mestizos, Blacks and mulattos do greatly molest us. We also implore you that no one take our government and jurisdiction from us. If it is thought we do not know how to rule, govern, and do true justice, let such laws be made for us as are necessary so that we can perform our duties properly, and if we do not observe them let us be punished. Let the right to rule which belongs to those who will follow us not be taken from them.

And if it is thought that we do not love the ruler and King of Castile, to put your mind to rest we here take oath as rulers, all of us who govern your city of Mexico; we who write this letter swear and take oath as rulers before God and St. Mary and all the saints and before you our ruler that we will always love, obey, and revere the ruler and king of Castile until the end of the world. And we

29

want this oath to hold for those who are born after us, and so that this our statement and rulers' oath will be valid we set down here are names and signatures.

Done here in Mexico City on December 19, 1554.

Your poor vassals who kiss your precious hands and feet.

Don Esteban de Guzmán, judge. Don Pedro de Motecuçoma. Don Diego de Mendoza, alcalde. Francisco de San Pablo, alcalde. Don Pedro de la Cruz, regidor. Don Luis de Paz, regidor. Bartolomé de San Juan, regidor. Don Baltasar Tlillancalqui, regidor. Diego Tezcacoacatl, regidor. Martín Cano, regidor. Martín Coçotecatl, regidor. Francisco Jiménez, regidor. Martín Tlamacicatl, regidor.


Source: Unpublished document, translated from the Nahuatl by James Lockhart.

## Equiano: A Slave En Route to the New World

The first object which saluted my eyes when I arrived on the coast was the sea, and a slave ship which was then riding at anchor and waiting for its cargo. These filled me with astonishment, which was soon converted into terror when I was carried on board. I was immediately handled and tossed up to see if I were sound by some of the crew, and I was now persuaded that I had gotten into a world of bad spirits and that they were going to kill me. Their complexions, too, differing so much from ours, their long hair and the language they spoke (which was very different from any I had every heard) united to confirm me in this belief. Indeed, such were the horrors of my views and fears at that moment that, if ten thousand worlds had been my own, I would have freely parted with them all to have exchanged my condition with that of the meanest slave in my own country.

I was soon put down under the decks, and there I received such a salutation to my nostrils as I had never experienced in my life: so that with the loathsomeness of the stench and crying together, I became so sick and low that I was not able to eat, nor had I the least desire to taste anything. I now wished for the last friend, death, to relieve me; but soon, to my grief, two of the white men offered me eatables, and on my refusing to eat, one of them held me fast by the hands and laid me across the windlass, and tied my feet while the other flogged me severely. I had never experienced anything like this before, and although not being used to the water, nevertheless could I have got over the nettings I would have jumped over the side.

The story of Olaudah Equiano, a slave from Nigeria

31

Source: *Equiano's Travels: His Autobiography*, Paul Edwards, ed. Oxford:

Heinemann International, 1989, 25-26.

# CHAPTER 3: INDEPENDENCE

Not all was peaceful in the Spanish colonies before the independence wars.

Among the uprisings to threaten the empire in the late colonial period was the

movement led in Peru by a mestizo, José Gabriel Condorcanqui Noguera, who

took the name Túpac Amaru. He appealed to indigenous, mestizos and creoles

by stressing to each the burdens that colonialism imposed on their communities.

The revolt began in November 1780 and was suppressed in January 1781. Here

we have two views of Condorcanqui, one from the *fiscal* (prosecuting attorney)

for the viceroyalty of Buenos Aires, and a very different one from

Condorcanqui's wife and chief aide, Micaela Bastidas Puyucahua, who played

in the ill-fated uprising. When the revolt was finally suppressed, Micaela was

sentenced to have her tongue cut out and to be strangled in front of

her husband.

Spain would not be successful in suppressing subsequent uprisings,

with all but Cuba and Puerto Rico winning their independence by 1824. One of

the major figures in these was was Simón Bolívar, often regarded as the father

of Latin American independence. Born in Caracas, Venezuela, he was a

member of the Caracas junta that rose up against Spanish rule. After the king

was restored and independence forces were defeated, he went into exile in

Jamaica. He returned to Latin America in 1816, where he successfully led the

independence movement in what became Colombia, Venezuela, Ecuador and

Peru. In the Jamaica letter, he responds to a query about the independence

movement by describing its causes and possible future.

# On Túpac Amaru: The Fiscal Speaks

What is worthy of attention in this affair is not so much the pitiful death of the *corregidor* Don Antonio de Arriaga, the theft of his fortune, the seizure of the arms that he had in his house, or the outrages committed bv the perfidious Túpac-Amaru, as the astuteness, the painstaking care and the deceptions with which he managed to perform and to subvert that and other provinces, preparing them to carry out his reprehensible secret designs.

It appears that in order to seize the *corregidor* Arriaga, in his own house, he arranged a banquet for his victim. In order to summon the military chiefs, caciques, and Indians of the provinces he compelled she unhappy *corregidor* to issue or sign orders to that effect. In order to drag him to the gallows in the presence of the multitude with no disturbance, he published a decree, pretending that he acted on His Majesty's orders. On the same pretext, after this horrible deed, he departed for the neighboring province of Quisicanchi, order to perpetrate similar atrocities on the *corregidor* and as many Spaniards as he could find, and as soon as he had returned to his town of Tungasuca issued orders to the caciques of neighboring provinces to imitate his example.

But the essence of the careful planning and perfidy of the traitor Tupac-Amaru consists in this, that after speaking so often of the royal orders which authorized him to proceed against the corregidores and other Europeans, in his orders, letters, and messages, and in the edicts which he dispatched to Don Diego Chuquiguanca, in order to revolutionize the province and Carabaya, he now says nothing about the orders of the king, and proceeds as the most distinguished Indian of the royal blood and principal line of the Incas to liberate his countrymen from the injuries, injustices, and slavery which the European

34

corregidores had inflicted on them, while the superior courts turned a deaf ear to their complaints. From which it follows that he repeatedly used the name of the king—in a vague way, not specifying our present ruler, Charles III—only to secure the acquiescence of the natives of those provinces in the violence done to Arriaga and to induce them to do the same to other corregidores. And considering these aims partially achieved, he transforms himself from a royal commissioner into a redeemer from injustices and burdens, moved only by pity for his compatriots, preparing the way for them to acclaim him as king, or at least to support their benefactor with arms, until they have raised him to the defunct throne of the tyrannical pagan kings of Peru, which is doubtless the goal of his contrivings.

Actually, he has already succeeded in assembling a large number of Indians, as noted by Colonel Don Pedro la Vallina (who was his prisoner) in a letter contained in the file on this case—and with their aid, it is stated—he slew some 300 men who came out to halt his advance on Cuzco, and took their weapons to arm the rebels who follow him. He took these first successful steps in his titanic enterprise after certain other things had occurred: the rising that took place in Arequipa as a result of the establishment of a customs house; the rioting that with less cause broke out in the city of La Paz; the disturbances that occurred in the provinces of Chayanta for the same reason; and the rumors that the natives in other provinces were somewhat restless.

When one considers that the rebel Tupac-Amaru, informed of these events, offers the natives freedom, not only from customs house duties but sales taxes, tributes, and forced labor in the mines, it must be admitted he offers them a powerful inducement to follow him1 and that there is imminent danger that the party of rebellion will progressively increase unless most energetic effort is made to slay this insolent rebel, the prime mover this conspiracy, so that others may be deterred from joining the rebellion and abandoning their loyalty to their legitimate monarch and natural lord, to the detriment of themselves and their commonwealth.

Source: *Visita del fiscal del virreinato de Buenos Aires, enero* 15 de 1781, in Manuel de Odriozola, ed., *Documentos históricos del Perú, Lima*, 1863, 123-133. Reprinted in *Latin American Civilization: History & Society, 1492 to the Present.* 6th ed. Benjamin Keen, ed. and tran. (Boulder, CO: Westview Press, 1996), 141-143.

## On Túpac Amaru: A Wife Speaks

Dear Chepe:

You are causing me grief and sorrow. While you saunter through the villages, even very carelessly delaying two days in Yauri, our soldiers rightly grow tired and are leaving for
their homes.

I do not have any patience left to endure all this. I am capable of giving myself up to the enemy and letting them take my life, because I see how lightly you view this grave matter that threatens the lives of all. We are in the midst of enemies and we have no security. And for your sake all my sons are in danger, as well as all our people.

I have warned you sufficient times against dallying in those villages where there is nothing to be done. But you continue to saunter without considering that the soldiers lack food supplies even though they are given money; and their pay will run out soon. Then they will all depart, leaving us helpless, and we will pay with our lives because they (as you must have learned) only follow self-interest and want to get all they can out of us. Now the soldiers are already beginning to desert; the soldiers are terrified and seek to flee, fearing the punishment that might befall them. Thus we will lose all the people I have gathered and prepared for the descent on Cuzco, and the Cuzco forces will unite with the troops from Lima who have already been on the march against us for many days.

I must caution you about all this, though it pains me. But if you wish to ruin us, you can just sleep. You were so careless that you walked alone through the streets of the town of Yauri, and even went to the extreme of climbing the church tower, when you should not commit such extreme actions under the present conditions. These actions only dishonor and even defame you and do you little justice.

I believed that you were occupied day and night in arranging these affairs, instead of showing an unconcern that robs me of my life. I am only a shadow of myself and beside myself with anxiety, and so I beg you to get on with this business.

You made me a promise, but from now on I shall not place any faith in your promises, for you did not keep your word.

I do not care about my own life, only about those of our poor family, who need all my help. Thus, if the enemy comes from Paruro, as I suggested in my last letter, I am prepared to march out to meet them with our forces, leaving Fernando in a designated place, for the Indians are not capable of moving by themselves in these perilous times.

I gave you plenty of warnings to march on Cuzco immediately, but you took them all lightly, allowing the enemy sufficient time to prepare, as they have done, placing cannon on Picchu mountain, plus other trickery so dangerous that you are no longer in a position to attack them. God keep you many years.

Tungasuca, December 6, 1780.

I must also tell you that the Indians of Quispicanchi are worn out and weary from serving so long as guards. Well, God must want me to suffer for my sins.

*Your wife.*

38

After I finished this letter, a messenger arrived with the news that the enemy from Paruro are in Archos. I shall march out to meet them though it cost me my life.

Source: *Martíres y heroínas,* Francisco A. Loáyza, ed. (Lima: Impresa D. Miranda, 1945), 48-51. Reprinted in *Women in Latin American History: their lives and views,* June E. Hahner, ed. Los Angeles: UCLA Latin American Center Publications, 1980, 36-37.

# Simón Bolívar: The Jamaica Letter

Kingston, Jamaica, September 6, 1815

My dear Sir:

I hasten to reply to the letter of the 29th ultimo which you had the honor of sending me and which I received with the greatest satisfaction.

Sensible though I am of the interest you desire to take in the fate of my country, and of your commiseration with her for the tortures she has suffered from the time of her discovery until the present at the hands of her destroyers, the Spaniards, I am no less sensible of the obligation which your solicitous inquiries about the principal objects of American policy place upon me. Every conjecture relative to America's future is, I feel, pure speculation. When mankind was in its infancy, steeped in uncertainty, ignorance and error, was it possible to foresee what system it would adopt for its preservation? Who could venture to say that a certain nation would be a republic or a monarchy; this nation great, that nation small? To my way of thinking, such is our situation. We are a young people. We inhabit a world apart, separated by broad seas. We are young in the ways of almost all the arts and sciences, although, in a certain manner, we are old in the ways of civilized society. I look upon the present state of America as similar to that of Rome after its fall. Each part of Rome adopted a political system conforming to its interest and situation or was led by the individual ambitions of certain chiefs, dynasties, or associations. But this important difference exists: those dispersed parts later reestablished their ancient nations, subject to the changes imposed by circumstances or events. But we scarcely retain a vestige of what once was; we are, moreover, neither Indian nor European, but a species midway between the legitimate proprietors of this country and the Spanish usurpers. In short, though American by birth we derive our rights from Europe, and we have to assert these rights against the rights of the natives, and at the same time we must defend ourselves against the invaders.

The role of the inhabitants of the American hemisphere has for centuries been purely passive. Politically they were non-existent. We are still in a position lower than slavery, and therefore it is more difficult for us to rise to the enjoyment of freedom. States are slaves because of either the nature or the misuse of their constitution; a people is therefore enslaved when the government, by its nature or its vices, infringes on and usurps the rights of the citizen or subject. Applying these principles, we find that America was denied not only its freedom but even an active and effective tyranny.

We have been harassed by a conduct which has not only deprived us of our rights but has kept us in a sort of permanent infancy with regard to public affairs. If we could at least have managed our domestic affairs and our internal administration, we could have acquainted ourselves with the processes and mechanics of public affairs. We should also have enjoyed a personal consideration, thereby commanding a certain unconscious respect from the people, which is so necessary to preserve amidst revolutions. That is why I say we have even been deprived of an active tyranny, since we have not been permitted to exercise its functions.

Americans today, and perhaps to a greater extent than ever before, who live within the Spanish system occupy a position in society no better than that of serfs destined for labor, or at best they have no more status than that of mere consumers. Yet even this status is surrounded with galling restrictions, such as being forbidden to grow European crops, or to store products which are royal monopolies, or to establish factories of a type the Peninsula itself does not possess. To this add the exclusive trading privileges, even in articles of prime necessity, and the barriers between American provinces, designed to prevent all exchange of trade, traffic, and understanding. In short, do you wish to know what our future held?—simply the cultivation of the fields of indigo, grain, coffee, sugar cane, cacao, and cotton; cattle raising on the broad plains; hunting wild game in the jungles; digging in the earth to mine its gold—but even these limitations could never satisfy the greed of Spain.

So negative was our existence that I can find nothing comparable in any other civilized society, examine as I may the entire history of time and the politics of all nations. Is it not an outrage and a violation of human rights to expect a land so splendidly endowed, so vast, rich, and populous, to remain merely passive?

As I have just explained, we were cut off, and, as it were, removed from the world in relation to the science of government and administration of the state. We were never viceroys or governors, save in the rarest of instances; seldom archbishops and bishops; diplomats never; as military men, only subordinate; as nobles, without royal privileges. In brief, we were neither magistrates nor financiers and seldom merchants—all in flagrant contradiction to our institutions.

Emperor Charles V made a pact with the discoverers, conquerors, and settlers of America, and this, as Guerra puts it, is our social contract. The monarchs of Spain made a solemn agreement with them, to be carried out on their own account and at their own risk, expressly prohibiting them from drawing on the royal treasury. In return, they were made the lords of the land,

42

entitled to organize the public administration and act as the court of last appeal, together with many other exemptions and privileges that are too numerous to mention. The King committed himself never to alienate the American provinces, inasmuch as he had no jurisdiction but that of sovereign domain. Thus, for themselves and their descendants, the *conquistadores* possessed what were tantamount to feudal holdings. Yet there are explicit laws respecting employment in civil, ecclesiastical, and tax-raising establishments These laws favor, almost exclusively, the natives of the country who are of Spanish extraction. Thus, by an outright violation of the laws and the existing agreements, those born in America have been despoiled of the constitutional rights as embodied in the code.

Events in Costa Firme have proved that institutions which are wholly representative are not suited to our character, customs, and present knowledge. As long as our countrymen do not acquire the abilities and political virtues that distinguish our brothers of the north, wholly popular systems, far from working to our advantage, will, I greatly fear, bring about our downfall. Unfortunately, these traits, to the degree in which they are required, do not appear to be within our reach. On the contrary, we are dominated by the vices that one learns under the rule of a nation like Spain, which has only distinguished itself in ferocity, ambition, vindictiveness and greed.

It is harder, Montesquieu has written, to release a nation from servitude than to enslave a free nation. Despite the convictions of history, South Americans have made efforts to obtain liberal, even perfect, institutions, doubtless out of that instinct to aspire to the greatest possible happiness, which, common to all men, is bound to follow in civil societies founded on the

43

principles of justice, liberty, and equality. But are we capable of maintaining in proper balance the difficult charge of a republic? Is it conceivable that a newly emancipated people can soar to the heights of liberty, and, unlike Icarus, neither have its wings melt nor fall into an abyss? Such a marvel is inconceivable and without precedent. There is no reasonable probability to bolster our hopes.

The American provinces are fighting for their freedom, and they will ultimately succeed. Some provinces as a matter of course will form federal and some central republics; the larger ones will inevitably establish monarchies, some of which will fare so badly that they will disintegrate in either present or future revolutions. To consolidate a great monarchy will be no easy task, but it will be utterly impossible to consolidate a great republic.

It is a grandiose idea to think of consolidating the New World into a single nation, united by pacts into a single bond. It is reasoned that, as these parts have a common origin, language, customs, and religion, they ought to have a single government to permit the newly–formed states to unite in a confederation. But this is not possible. Actually, America is separated by climatic differences, geographic diversity, conflicting interests, and dissimilar characteristics.

Among the popular and representative systems, I do not favor the federal system. It is over-perfect, and it demands political virtues and talents far superior to our own. For the same reason I reject a monarchy that is part aristocracy and part democracy, although with such a government England has achieved much fortune and splendor. Since it is not possible for us to select the most perfect and complete form of government, let us avoid falling into demagogic anarchy or monocratic tyranny. These opposite extremes would only wreck us on similar reefs of misfortune and dishonor; hence, we must seek a mean between them. I say: Do not adopt the best system of government, but the one that is most likely to succeed.

Surely, unity is what we need to complete our work of regeneration. The division among us, nevertheless, is nothing extraordinary, for it is characteristic of civil wars to form two parties, *conservatives* and *reformers*. The former are commonly the more numerous, because the weight of habit induces obedience to established powers; the latter are always fewer in number although more vocal and learned. Thus, the physical mass of the one is counterbalanced by the moral force of the other; the contest is prolonged, and the results are uncertain. Fortunately, in our case, the mass has followed the learned.

I shall tell you with what we must provide ourselves in order to expel the Spaniards and to found a free government. It is *union*, obviously; but such union will come about through sensible planning and well-directed actions rather than by divine magic. America stands together because it is abandoned by all other nations. It is isolated in the center of the world. It has no diplomatic relations, nor does it receive any military assistance; instead, America is attacked by Spain, which has more military supplies than any we can possibly acquire through furtive means.

When success is not assured, when the state is weak, and when results are distantly seen, all men hesitate; opinion is divided, passions rage, and the enemy fans these passions in order to win an easy victory because of them. As soon as we are strong and under the guidance of a liberal nation which will lend us her protection, we will achieve accord in cultivating the virtues and talents that lead to glory. Then will we march majestically toward that great prosperity for which South America is destined. Then will those sciences and arts which, born in the East, have enlightened Europe, wing their way to a free Colombia, which will cordially bid

them welcome.

Such, Sir, are the thoughts and observations that I have the honor to submit to you, so that you may accept or reject them according to their merit. I beg you to understand that I have expounded them because I do not wish to appear discourteous and not because I consider myself competent to enlighten you concerning these matters.

I am, Sir...Simón Bolívar

Source: *Selected Writings of Bolívar*, compiled by Vicente Lecuna, ed Harold A. Bierck Jr. (NY: Bolivarian Society of Venezuela, 1951) 103-122; reprinted in *People and Issues in Latin American History*. Lewis Hanke and Jane M. Rausch, eds. (N.Y.: Markus Wiener Publishing, Inc., 1992), 17-26.

# CHAPTER 4: EARLY REPUBLICS

No two authors sum up the struggles of the early republic better than Domingo

Faustino Sarmiento (1811-1888) and José Hernandez. Sarmiento was among

the foremost liberal reformers and authors of the nineteenth century. He was a

tireless opponent of the caudillo Juan Manuel de Rosas, a follower of Horace

Mann who advocated for widespread education, and served as president of

Argentina from 1868-1874. In his most famous work, *Facundo o la civilización*

*y barbarie*, he articulates the liberal, elite preference for an urban, Europeanized

way of life.

In contrast, José Hernández (1834-1886) reclaimed the image of the

gaucho with his epic poem Martín Fierro, published in 1872 and 1879. Contrary

to Sarmiento's views of the gaucho as barbarian, Hernández gives us the honest

man, the soul of Argentina, put upon by the corrupt forces of government and

business. Long after the gaucho ceased to be a threat in the eyes of leaders like

Sarmiento, the image of the gaucho as presented by Hernández would become a

symbol of Argentina.

Views such as Sarmiento's were common throughout Latin America

and were often expressed in concern about race. As we see in a circular sent by

the federal government in preparation for a census in Nicaragua in 1883, the

issue of race was of primary concern.

## Domingo F. Sarmiento, *Civilization and Barbarism*

The people who inhabit these extensive districts belong to two different races, the Spanish and the native; the combinations of which form a series of imperceptible gradations. The pure Spanish race predominates in the rural districts of Cordova and San Luis, where it is common to met young shepherdesses fair and rosy, and as beautiful as the belles of a capital could wish to be. In Santiago del Estero, the bulk of the rural population still speaks the Quichua dialect, which plainly shows its Indian origin. The country people of Corrientes use a very pretty Spanish dialect. The Andalusian soldier may still be recognized in the rural districts of Buenos Aires; and in the city foreign surnames are the most numerous. The negro race, by this time nearly extinct (except in Buenos Aires), has left, in its zambos and mulattos, a link which connects civilized man with the denizen of the woods. This race mostly inhabiting cities, has a tendency to become civilized, and possesses talent and the finest instincts of progress.

With these reservations, a homogenous whole has resulted from the fusion of the three above-named families. It is characterized by love of idleness and incapacity for industry, except when education and the exigencies of a social position succeed in spurring it out of its customary pace. To a great extent, this unfortunate result is owing to the incorporation of the native tribes, effected by the process of colonization. The American aborigines live in idleness, and show themselves incapable, even under compulsion, of hard and protracted labor. This suggested the idea of introducing negroes into America, which has produced such fatal results. But the Spanish race has not shown itself more energetic than the aborigines, when it has been left to its own instincts in the wilds of America. Pity and shame are excited by the comparison of one of the German or Scotch colonies in the southern part of Buenos Ayres and some towns of the interior of the Argentine Republic; in the former the cottages are painted, the frontyards always neatly kept and adorned with flowers and pretty shrubs; the furniture simple but complete; copper or tin utensils always bright and clean; nicely curtained beds; and the occupants of the dwelling are always industriously at work. Some such families have retired to enjoy the conveniences of city life, with great fortunes gained by their previous labors in milking their cows, and making butter and cheese. The town inhabited by natives of the country presents a picture entirely the reverse. There, dirty and ragged children live, with a menagerie of dogs; there, men lie about in utter idleness; neglect and poverty prevail everywhere; a table and some baskets are the only furniture of wretched huts remarkable for their general aspect of barbarism and carelessness.

The Argentine cities, like almost all the cities of South America, have an appearance of regularity. Their streets are laid out at right angles, and their population scattered over a wide surface, except in Cordova, which occupies a narrow and confined position, and presents all the appearance of a European city, the resemblance being increased by the multitude of towers and domes attached to its numerous and magnificent churches. All civilization, whether native, Spanish, or European, centers in the cities, where are to be found the manufactories, the shops, the schools and colleges, and other characteristics of civilized nations. Elegance of style, articles of luxury, dress-coats, and frocked-coats, with other European garments, occupy their appropriate place in these towns. I mention these small matters designedly. It is sometimes the case that the only city of a pastoral province is its capital, and occasionally the land is uncultivated up to its very streets. The encircling desert besets such cities at a greater or less distance, and bears heavily upon them, and they are thus small oases of civilization surrounded by an untilled plain, hundreds of square miles in extent, the surface of which is but rarely interrupted by any settlement of consequence.

The cities of Buenos Aires and Cordova have succeeded better than the others in establishing about them subordinate towns to serve as new foci of civilization and municipal interests; a fact which deserves notice. The inhabitants of the city wear the European dress, live in a civilized manner, and possess laws, ideas of progress, means of instruction, some municipal organization, regular forms of government, etc. Beyond the precincts of the city everything assumes a new aspect; the country people wear a different dress, which I will call South American, as it is common to all districts; their habits of life are different, their wants peculiar and limited. The people composing these two distinct forms of society do not seem to belong to the same nation. Moreover, the countryman, far from attempting to imitate the customs of the city, rejects with disdain its luxury and refinement; and is unsafe for the costume of the city people, their coats, their cloaks, their saddles, or anything European, to show themselves in the country. Everything civilized which the city contains is blockaded there, proscribed beyond its limits; and any one who should dare to appear in the rural districts in a frock-coat, for example, or mounted on an English saddle, would bring ridicule and brutal assaults upon himself.

The whole remaining population inhabit the open country, which, whether wooded or destitute of the large plants, is generally level, and almost everywhere occupied by pastures, in some places of such abundance and excellence, that the grass of an artificial meadow would not surpass them. Mendoza and especially San Juan are exceptions to this general absence of tilled fields, the people here depending chiefly on the products of agriculture. Everywhere else, pasturage being plenty, the means of subsistence of the inhabitants--for we cannot call it their occupation--is stock-raising. Pastoral life reminds us of the Asiatic plains, which imagination covers with Kalmuck, Cossack or Arab tents. The primitive life of nations--a life essentially barbarous and unprogressive--the life of Abraham, which is that of the Bedouin of today, prevails in the Argentine plains, although modified in a peculiar manner by civilization. The Arab tribe which wanders through the wilds of Asia, is united under the rule of one of its elders or of a warrior chief; society exists, although not fixed in any determined locality. Its religious opinions, immemorial traditions, unchanging customs, and its sentiments of respect for the aged, make altogether a code of laws and a form of government which preserves morality, as it is there understood, as well as order and the association of the tribe. But progress is impossible, because there can be no progress without permanent possession of the soil, or without cities, which are the means of developing the capacity of man for the processes of industry, and which enable him to extend his acquisitions.

Before 1810, two distinct, rival, and incompatible forms of society, two differing kinds of civilization existed in the Argentine Republic: one being Spanish, European, and cultivated, the other barbarous, American, and almost wholly of native growth. The revolution (1810) which occurred in the cities acted only as the cause, the impulse, which set these two distinct forms of national existence face-to-face, and gave occasion for a contest between them, to be ended, after lasting many years, by the absorption of one into the other.

I have pointed out the normal form of association, or want of association, of the country people, a form worse, a thousand times, than that of the nomad tribe. I have described the artificial associations formed in idleness, and the sources of fame among the gauchos—bravery, daring, violence, and opposition to regular law, to the civil law, that is, of the city. These phenomena of social organization existed in 1810, and still exist, modified in many points, slowly changing in others, and yet untouched in several more. These foci, about which were gathered the brave, ignorant, free, and unemployed peasantry, were found by thousands through the country. The revolution of 1810 carried everywhere commotion and the sound of arms. Public life, previously wanting in this Arabico-Roman society, made its appearance in all the taverns, and the revolutionary movement finally brought about provincial, warlike associations, called *montoneras*, legitimate of offspring of the tavern and the field, hostile to the city and to the army of revolutionary patriots. As events succeed each other, we shall see the provincial montoneras headed by their chiefs; the final triumph, in Facundo Quiroga, of the country over the cities.

Throughout the land; and by their subjugation in spirit, government, and civilization, the final formation of the central consolidated despotic government of the landed proprietor, Don Juan Manuel Rosas, who applied the knife of the gaucho to the culture of Buenos Aires, and destroyed the work of centuriesof—civilization, law, and liberty.

Thus elevated, and hitherto flattered by fortune, Buenos Ayres set about making a constitution or itself and the Republic, just as it had undertaken

52

to liberate itself and all South America: that is, eagerly, uncompromisingly, and without regard to obstacles. Rivadavia was the personification of this poetical, utopian spirit which prevailed. He therefore continued the work of Las Heras upon the large scale necessary for a great American State—a republic. He brought over from Europe men of learning for the press and for the professor's chair, colonies for the deserts, ships for the rivers, freedom for all creeds, credit and the national bank to encourage trade, and all the great social theories of the day for the formation of government. In a word, he brought a second Europe, which was to be established in America, and to accomplish in ten years what elsewhere had required centuries. Nor was this project altogether chimerical; all his administrative creations still exist, except those which the barbarism of Rosas found in its way. Freedom of conscience, advocated by the chief clergy of Buenos Aires, has not been repressed; the European population is scattered on farms throughout the country, and takes arms of its own accord to resist the only obstacle in the way of the wealth offered by the soil. The rivers only need to be freed from governmental restrictions to become navigable, and the national bank, them firmly established, has saved the people from the poverty to which the tyrant would have brought them. And, above all, however fanciful and impracticable that great system of government may have been, it was at least easy and endurable for the people; and, notwithstanding the assertions of misinformed men, Rivadavia never shed a drop of blood, nor destroyed the property of any one; but voluntarily descended from the Presidency to poverty and exile. Rosas, by whom he was so calumniated, might easily have been drowned in the blood of his won victims, and the forty millions of dollars from the national treasury, with the fifty millions from private fortunes which were consumed in ten years of the long war provoked by his brutalities, would have been employed by the *"fool*–the *dreamer*, Rivadavia,"* in building canals, cities, and useful public buildings. Then let this man, who died for his country, have the glory of representing the highest aspirations of European civilization, and leave to his adversaries that of displaying South American barbarism in its most odious light. For Rosas and Rivadavia are the two extremes of the Argentine Republic, connecting it with savages through the pampas, and with Europe through the river La Plata.

Ah! when will an impartial history of the Argentine Republic be written? And when will its people be able, without fear of a tyrant, to read the terrible drama of the revolution—the well-intentioned and brilliant, but chimerical government of Rivadavia; the power and brutal deeds of Facundo Quiroga; and the administration of Rosas, the great tyrant of the nineteenth century, who unconsciously revived the spirit of the Middle Ages, and the doctrine of equality armed with the knife of Danton and Robespierre. If we lack an intelligent population, let the people of Europe once feel that there is a permanent peace and freedom in our country, and multitudes of emigrants would find their way to a land where success is sure. No, we are not the lowest among Americans. Something is to result from this chaos; either something surpassing the government of the United States of North America, or something a thousand times worse than that of Russia,—the Dark Ages returned, or political institutions, superior to any yet known.

Source: Domingo F. Sarmiento, *Life in the Argentine Republic in the Days of the Tyrants: Or Civilization and Barbarism* (NY: Hafner, n.d.), 10-15, 54-55, 126-127, 246-247. Reprinted in *Latin America: Conflict and Creation: A Historical Reader.* E. Bradford Burns, ed. (Englewood Cliffs, NJ: Prentice Hall, 1993), 77-81.

## El Gaucho Martín Fierro

I am a gaucho, and take this from me

as my tongue explains to you:

for me the earth is a small place

and it could well be bigger–

the snake does not bite me

nor the sun burn my brow.


I was born as a fish is born

at the bottom of the sea;

no one can take from me

what I was given by God–

what I brought into the world

I shall take from the world with me.


It is my glory to life as free

as a bird in the sky:

I make no nest on this ground

where there's so much to be suffered,

and no one will follow me when I take flight again....


Let whoever may be listening

to the tale of my sorrows–

know that I never fight nor kill

except when it has to be done,

and that only injustice threw me

into so much adversity.


And listen to the story told

by a gaucho who's hunted by the law;

who's been a father and husband

hard-working and willing–

and in spite of that, people take him

to be a criminal.


In my part of the land, at one time,

I had children, cattle, and a wife;

but my sufferings began,

they pushed me out to the frontier–

and when I got back, what was I to find!

a ruin, and nothing more.


You couldn't call that service

nor defending the frontier,

it was more like a nest or rats

where the strongest one plays the cat–

it was like gambling with a loaded dice.


Everything here works the wrong way round,

soldiers turned into laborer

and go round the settlements

out on loan for work–

they join them up again to fight

when the Indian robbers break in.


In this merry-go-round, I've seen

many officers who owned land,

with plenty of work-hands

and herds of cattle and sheep–

I may not be educated

but I've seen some ugly deals.


I was returning after three years

of suffering so much for nothing,

a deserter, naked and penniless,

in search of a better life–

and like an armadillo

I headed straight for my den.


I found not a trace of my cabin–

there was only the empty shell.

Christ! if that wasn't a sight

to bring sorrow to your heart.

I swore at that moment

to be as pitiless as a wild beast.

I mounted, and trusting to God,

I made for another district–

because a gaucho they call a vagrant

can have no place of his own,

and so he lives from one trouble to the next

lamenting what he has lost.


He's always on the run,

always poor and hounded,

he has neither a hole nor a nest

as if there were a curse on him,

because being a gaucho . . . curse it,

being a gaucho is a crime.

# "I Must Insist on This Matter of Race."

Circular No. 4, Managua, May 18, 1883 Chief, Department of Statistics, Granada

I remit to you by this post 48 packets, with 50 copies in each of the forms to be used to conduct the general census of the Republic, which you will divide among the local agents of your department in proportion to the number of inhabitants of each town, keeping in mind that each copy has room for 31 individuals.

I believe it necessary to painstakingly call attention to the difficulty that certain columns on this form present to be able to fill in certain data that must not be left out.

There will be no difficulty whatsoever in the columns on age, sex, legitimacy or illegitimacy of birth, marital status (only single, married, and widowed), political capacity, religion, physical or moral impediment, and vaccination; but it will not be the same with race, profession, office and education because there are many elements to note, and they require very special care to not make errors.

The races that people Nicaragua are six types of classes that are fairly clear and can be easily known. These types are:

Pure while, pure Indian, pure negro, mestizo, mulato and zambo. The three first ones are well defined and offer no difficulty whatsoever to be determined. Regarding the mestizo, this is the result of the mix of Indian and white, just as the mulato is of white and black and the zambo is of black and Indian. These types are known in an individual by the mix of both elements that occur in their features, hair and color.

I must insist on this matter of race. I believe it indispensable that you emphasize these explanations to the local agents, taking into account their limited ability to understand because of the low culture. In fact, give them various examples, for instance, of this type: An individual of light black skin, very curly hair, a thick and short body, is evidently a zambo, the hair reveals the pure black, and the color and size the Indian.

As the census will be repeated every four years, it is necessary to know the race in each period and whether the proportion is rising or declining.

Your efforts could never be too strong in gathering this data with the greatest perfection possible.

Regarding education, this can be primary, intermediate or superior. Primary includes those that know how to read and write or have the instruction given in our public schools. Intermediate comprises those that have the cientific grade of bachelor's degree, whether in philosophy, law or in medicine. And superior would be those that have professional titles or who stand out notably in their scientific field, in which case in the column on education write, for example, botany or chemistry, if those were the branches in which the excelled. Nonetheless, in the column for profession or office, note the actual profession, so that if Manuel Gonzalez appears in the column indicating his education is in medicine, but his profession is farmer, what is being indicated is that this individual, although he possesses the diploma in medicine, does not work as a doctor but works and lives from agriculture, that being his real profession.

On this point, too, it seems to me that you should explain and clarify as much as possible so that it cannot be as easily hidden since local agents can confuse profession with education and vice versa.

61

I have little to say in regard to the last point, that is, profession or office, and I will limit myself to saying that what must be noted is the person's actual profession; and if someone has various professions or office, give preference to those that he exercises the most.

Source:  Archivo Municipal de la Prefectura de Granada.

# CHAPTER 5: THE EMERGENCE OF THE MODERN STATE

In the late nineteenth century, Liberals and Conservatives put aside many of their differences to unite on the economic project of modernizing their countries. One of the main forms of modernization was the introduction of railroads, which brought the produce of distant provinces to the ports, created a national market, and brought government officials and businessmen from the capitals to the provinces.

One of the leaders in the effort to modernize was Mexico's Porfirio Díaz, who oversaw a vast expansion in the country's railroad network, much of it owned by foreign investors. Díaz was criticized for turning much of the country over to foreigners. Here he is defended by Justo Sierra (1848-1912), a Mexican educator and liberal reformer who served as Díaz's minister of education.

A dramatically, perhaps melodramatically, different view is presented by Argentine author Ricardo Güiraldes (1886-1927) in the short story "Rosaura," published in 1922. Unlike his countryman Sarmiento, Güiraldes saw the Argentine countryside as the soul of the nation, at risk of being destroyed by the march of "civilization," symbolized by the train. His story helped propel a national debate about how much modernity should be imported, and how much of what was truly national should be preserved.

## Justo Sierra: In Support of Porfirio Díaz

The country's real desire, manifested everywhere, was peace. No one wanted a resumption of the war except those who thrived on anarchy, those who were misfits in any normal situation. Seldom in history has there been a people with a more unanimous, more anguished, more determined aspiration.

In order to make this seemingly visionary ideal a reality, all interests, from the highest to the lowest must be involved, and the leader believed that, to accomplish this, all must have faith in him and fear him. Faith and fear, those two profoundly human emotions, have been the pillars of every religion and were to be the pillars of the new political regime. Without losing a day or wasting an opportunity, President Díaz has marched in this direction for twenty-five years: he has founded the political religion of peace.

Never before had peace been so patently a matter of urgent national necessity. The industrial development of the United States, already colossal twenty-five years ago, required a concomitant development of the railroad system, for without this it ran the risk of paralysis, something American "go-ahead" could never permit. The builders of the great systems that approached our frontiers planned to complete them in Mexico, which was regarded by the communication experts as forming a single region with the southwestern United States. The financial object of the Americans in extending their railway network to Mexico was to dominate our markets to the profit of their industry. This American need could be satisfied by declaring the country to be in a state of anarchy and intervening to give the railroad builders protection, or it could be satisfied in a normal, pacific manner if they could be convinced that there was a stable and viable government in Mexico whose word in treaties and contracts could be trusted. From this moment, civil war could be considered not only as the gravest of the country's internal ills, but also as responsible for attracting the most imminent external danger. Lerdo had tried to forestall this danger by seeking the concurrence of European capital, but to no avail. European capital would come to Mexico only after long years, and then as backing for American enterprises. President Díaz had the perspicacity to understand the situation and, believing that our history and the state of our society put us in a position where we were liable to be hooked and carried off into the future by the formidable Yankee locomotive, he preferred to make that journey under the auspices and through the action of the Mexican government, as equal partners with the obligation to preserve peace and order, thereby maintaining our national integrity and achieving progress.

Many who have tried to analyze the psyche of President Díaz—who, without being either an archangel or a tyrant of melodrama, is in the true sense of the word an extraordinary man—find in his mental processes a notable inversion of logic: his decisions are quick, and deliberation follows the act of will, deliberation that is slow and laborious and modifies or even nullifies the original decision. This mental pattern, characteristic, perhaps, of the mixed family to which the majority of Mexicans belong, has given rise to imputations of political perfidy (deceiving in order to persuade, dividing in order to rule). These imputations, contradicted by the qualities that we all recognize in the private man, are mechanisms by which some individuals in Mexican society attain contact with power and identify with the powerful. This society has inherited from the idiosyncracies of the indigenous race, from colonial education, and from the perennial anarchy of the epochs of revolt an infinite

65

distrust of rulers and all their acts; what we criticize, no doubt, is the reflection of ourselves in the other person. We needed a man, a conscience, a will to unify our moral forces and transmute them into national progress; this man was President Díaz.

But if we compare Mexico's situation at the instant when the parenthesis in her political evolution was opened with the present moment, we must admit that the transformation has been amazing. Only we who were witnesses of preceding events can fully appreciate the change.

A peace lasting from ten to twenty years was an idle dream, they said. But ours has already lasted a quarter of a century. It was mere dreaming, they said, to think of covering the country with a railway system that would unite the ports and the center with the hinterland and the outside world. Only in a dream would one see a national industry in rapid growth. But all these things have come true, and still we move forward.

The undeniable achievement of the present administration consists, not in having brought about this change, which an extraneous combination of factors would probably have brought anyway, but in having done everything possible to facilitate the change and exploit it to the best advantage. In the course of this task, nothing has been more beneficial to the country than the intimate collaboration between the President's firm resolution and his Finance Minister's application of scientific procedures to financial problems. To this collaboration we owe the revival of our credit, the balancing of our budget, the freedom of internal trade, and the concomitant increase in public revenue.

There exists, we repeat, such a thing as Mexican social evolution. Our progress, made up of foreign elements, reveals, on analysis, a reaction of our

66

social body to those elements in order to assimilate and make use of them in developing and intensifying our life. Thus, our national personality has been enriched and made stronger by contact with the world. This evolution, no doubt, is just beginning. When we look back at our condition previous to the final third of the past century we see what a long way we have come, and even if we compare our progress with that made by our neighbors (and this should always be our frame of reference, without succumbing to pernicious illusions or to cowardly discouragement) it is not insignificant.

Source: From THE POLITICAL EVOLUTION OF THE MEXICAN PEOPLE by Justo Sierra, translated by Charles Ramsdell, Copyright (c) 1969. By permission of the University of Texas Press.

# The Darker Side of Modernization: "Rosaura"

I.

Lobos is a tranquil town, in the middle of the pampa.

An indifferent boredom drifts through its tree-fringed streets.

Few passersby sound on its pavements, steps tell-tale as hoof beats, and except at the train hour or during the summer promenades on the plaza, fresh with evening quiet, nothing stirs the sober siesta which a spinster conscience seems to impose on the town's friendliness.

Like all our towns, Lobos possesses a plaza whose blunt brick enclosure, exposed by a recent sacrifice of old vines, stretches across from the Church, and daily flaunts an artificial sleekness renewed by the long and flexible nozzle of a hose.

The Church is colonial style, its great courtyard of red flags rimmed with a single zigzag marble parquet. In front, the plaza between, is the police station with its coat-of-arms and its chief in view, while his orderly takes the air to the count of *mates* prepared by an ex-felon policeman, who trades retail in pardons.

A two-story branch of the Banco de la Nación overlooks one of the corners of the square. On the second corner, counting by display, the gastronomic windows of the Jardin confectionery, known by residents familiarly as "the Basque's," spread out an invitation for the afternoon. And while on the third, the store smiles percaline brightness, on the fourth the pharmacy reminds that here are ills in this world.

Here is all the community needs: justice, money, clothing, self-indulgence, and ideals—in moderate doses.

68

The main artery of the town's life, one of the streets opening into the plaza, is called *Calle Real* and is cobblestoned. Ornate souvenirs of some Louis on its houses are tempered by massive old elms in danger of being felled by a progressive administration which might not consider them fine trees.

In a row, monopolizing the privilege of the pavement noisy under wheels and hoofs, stand the Hotel de Paris, the Club Social, the *Globo* Jewelry, the clothing store, and the *Modelo* shoe shop.

Five or six blocks from this center, the squares of monotonous colourless structures built adjoining are brightened here and there by a bush or a tree whose serene crown looks out over the dusty bricks of the walls, flat and angular as a house of cards. The facades begin to glow yellows, greens, and sky blues, blotting paper tones. Doors and windows are framed in deeper hues. Through doorways a glimpse of vines is caught reflected in polished tile floors.

On the fringe, the grocery store, once the headquarters for the alley, sleeps deserted, despite the mildly-domestic air lent by a sorry team of hacks (one grey, the other dappled) dozing harnessed to a springwagon.

Villas scatter the town into a vast horizon of ranches, to which summer visitors bring the only glitter of wealth in the district.

The soul of Lobos was simple and primitive as a red bloom. Lobos thought, loved, lived, in its own way. Then came the parallel infinities of swift rails, and the train, marching armoured to indifference from horizon to horizon, from stranger to stranger, brushed its passing plume over the settlement.

Lobos fell ill of that poison.

II.

In a car of the National Railways that afternoon rode a young man dressed in European style, irreproachably: collar and tie, soft hat, and country suit that, though worn, retained in the lining of an inner pocket the label and date of delivery from Poole. His legs were encased almost to the knee in boots impeccably curved. Beside him balainced a suitcase from a great London house, colorfully patched with stickers that recorded stays at fashionable hotels and beaches. His coat hung from the clumsy rack. And the thick-seamed gloves lay like a pair of amputated Indian hands on the dusty table in the middle of which a litre of water danced spherically within a round-bellied jug of long and pretentious neck.

The youth's clothing proclaimed an education abroad. His dark skin, evenly-laid either side of a lean nose, his high and rigidly correct bearing, revealed Castilian descent; something silent and searching in his pupils several generations of watchful pampa life; and the native zest of a new race braced his easy laughter.

The Inspector called him Don Carlos when he asked for the tickets. His age might have been gauged roughly as somewhere between twenty-five and thirty. With leisure, he glanced through a daily, at the cattle market quotations.

The cars jarred abruptly, the asthmatic gasps of the locomotive died down, a yellow lantern illegibly flashed past, the earth-level rose to a platform outlined by a row of banana trees; the train stopped in front of the lighted corridor of that station that shut out the night.

People descended, people ascended. The boiler hissed like a deflating balloon. The buzz of a bee hive rose from the crowd: politicians out

70

campaigning, fashionable youths in gray felts and light shoes, personages displaying their official personalities, sheiks with straw hats about to slide off their greasy foreheads and stickily-pomaded skulls, coachmen waiting for fares, *peons* for mail or on errands, while like perfume blossoms in the jungle, the exuberant girls of Lobos came and went shyly discreet or laughing excessively, nervous—who knows why.

Three went, arm in arm, slowly: one in sky blue, another in pink, another in yellow. Toward Carlos' window they glanced with such bold curiosity that he, annoyed, squared his shoulders, breathed high, and flushed aggressively and violently as a turkey. In defense he fixed his eyes upon one of them, thinking to intimidate, but instead the girl held that gaze as wood does a plug.

They passed. Two or three times they promenaded the station from end to end, walking with the careless ease of coquettes. Carlos, no longer offended, took the play and gazed after the swaying little figure retreating as if in anger, bored with his eyes into the pupils that became penetrable and docile.

And she with surprise felt her eyes opened like that, as if they had been careless windows, and her body overcome by a strange wave of languor.

But it was all play and when the train jerked out after a blazon of whistle and bell, as the elegant youth half-bowed, they laughed openly, correcting that rudeness with a bare and almost involuntary dip of the head to the shoulder.

The car passed quickly, striking from the station windows a vibrant echo.

III.

Her name was Rosaura Torres and she was the daughter of old man Crescencio,

owner of the wealthiest livery stables in town, an estate which counted no less

than five cabs drawn by horses splendid for work, God willing.

It was large, half a block, this place of brick and unwhitewashed clay.

The hallway, dining room, kitchen and bedrooms faced front. Inside

they backed by a porch from the eaves of which hung, like slim and long sensual

boas, intricate vines hungrily embracing. A tiny orchard containing one flower

tree, three fruit-bearers, and four small cottonwoods, flourished either side of a

grape arbor.

Enclosing this quiet ensemble, where the women trailed their skirts as

they went about their homely tasks, a wire fence upheld the subtle rustle of

honeysuckles and climbing roses.

The corral was nearly open field, with its light zinc roof to protect the

vehicles, harness and fodder, its little yard with stalls for the horses, its chicken

coop which used up the trough waste, and its adopted cur, not so harmless,

despite the whimperings and snugglings of the little fellow.

Her name was Rosaura Torres and she was pretty. Her slippers slapped

at indolently like oriental sandals; her hands were skilled, her laughter eager, her

dreams simple; life waited curious within her inviolate lips.

For her, every waking was gay, to live a daily boon, all flowers

beautiful, the afternoons smiling and tranquil with something that cradled and

soothed.

72

Rosaura was pretty and waiting to plunge her skilled hands into life, as into her morning basket of flowers.

IV.

She had two blocks to go along the narrow sidewalk a meter above the dusty road, to reach the main street.

Rosaura walked out about five-thirty in her yellow dress, generously powdered, enjoying to the full all the usual incidents of her pilgrimage to the station, where she waited like the others for the six-thirty-five express.

At five-thirty Rosaura would leave, unaware of the miracle of youth that went with her. She crossed the end of the street, careful not to make a misstep in her Louis XV heels, and not to smudge with sandy soil the mirror perfection of her shoes. Half a block down she exchanged a good afternoon with old Petrona, who always stood on the threshold of her white house, her arms pillowed on the soft mound of her stomach, shaken with deep laughter.

"Hello, Doña Petrona."

"God bless you, child . . . why, you're a regular doll . . . poor boys!"

Rosaura never heard the end, always crude banter, and she hurried the swift patter of her bright little shoes, knowing that at the corner masculine eyes would manage better to convey those flatteringly but repellent, thoughts.

She was on the main street. Fashionable Lobos promenaded between station and plaza, its greetings and laughter ruffling the earlier silence of the streets.

The minutes flicked by spent in chatter, salvaged by charming or important ends. Words cloaked the feelings of the men and women who brushed each other—the women with the air of jewels on display, the men like wary customers concealing their tastes.

The afternoon would be winding itself out in dark corners, when the promenade, aimless heretofore, turned toward the station. Planks creaked in the floor of the waiting room, through which the platform was gradually invaded.

And it was always the same, from the Bois de Boulogne with its tide of coughing motors to the modest echo of village heels, there in this last corner of the world, where tiny hopes waver up in a piteously simple society.

The station is to Lobos what Hyde Park is to London, the Retiro to Madrid, the Sweet Waters of Asia to Constantinople. If a slight, unknown guilt exists, it does not fall there.

But the first train is in. It is six o'clock, highest pitch of excitement till six-thirty-five, when the really important one, dealer of emotions from Buenos Aires, is due.

People passed, criticized, and a web of romanticism entangled the youth of the town.

The minutes scrambled down the restless clock.

Rosaura saw that fashionable young man many times. Her friends teased her because of the insistent glances that they perhaps wished for themselves, and the girl felt something agreeably clouding her reason, when Carlos looked at her smiling, watching for recognition.

An emotion, greater than the little breast in the yellow dress, welled in Rosaura.

Through the restless days that speed too, the hours come again and again, and among them the moment when the express is due. The initials of an

74

idyll can be traced on the dusty haunch of the cars, and Rosaura wrote her name on the diner, in which traveled the fashionable youth of the glance.

Oh, evil influence of the indifferent locomotive to whose monster eye the horizon presents no ideal! Pitiless train that passed on, abandoning to the monotonous boredom of the village those fanciful dreams of the sentimental Rosaura who wrote her fate on its cars!

But the enamoured child was too much a part of today's amazement to sense the disharmony between stable people and the great forces that pass. And one afternoon, when Carlos got down, ostensibly for a walk, and passed beside her very near, she felt she would fall, strangely drawn as if by the slight breath in his wake.

V.

Little garden with your arbour, your odorous jasmine, your white and cold laurel and sexual carnations, something stirs there to fill you so tenderly. In Rosaura the simple provincial of pastoral soul, blooms the miracle of a great love.

Rosaura lives closing her eyes to possess more completely her intense emotion. Her coquetry is wasted no longer: for him her arms drop in consent; for him her pupils suffer this concentrated feeling; for him her body yields unknown surrender, when she walks wrapped in disturbing daydreams; and for him too, her breast fills to the size of an entire world.

How enormous is this unsuspected world! At times Rosaura thinks and fears: What will be of her life now? Is this love? Does that incredibly elegant and distinguished youth love her too? She thinks and fears and leaves unsolved those impossible elusive problems.

Rosaura closes her eyes to possess more completely her intense emotion.

The days are no longer monotonous nor the hours leaden in that tiny unsuspected garden, there in the pampa that sings its endless song of the unending spaces.

And the spring that is not illusion brings the lilacs to bloom, clinging twined in clustered embraces, falling splendid in violet sprays; and in the vines that drooped from the eaves like slim and sensual boas, timid gleams of white jasmine appear. The honeysuckle breathes a hint of the tropics, vibrant as a ringing and the potted carnations burst into pride.

The soul of Rosaura wells an odour of troubled love like the perfumed wave of the honeysuckles. Her cheeks are like jasmine, her eyes become pooled to a sheen of grape, and her blood ripens her mouth so that she strangely needs to bite her lips.

The soul of Rosaura slowly is inhaled by her body.

VI.

Restlessly wandering about, Rosaura awaits the unrealized idyll of those glances. Will he come? Won't he come?

She pictures beforehand, in the square of light framed by the car window, that fine profile hastily looking up from the paper to seek her alone, among all the girls of the crowded platform.

Always it is his tense eyes that pierce her, fixed on her black locks, on her shoulders, on her walk which suddenly shifts with mysterious languor.

To look into his face is a physical shock and just to think of his face flushes her cheeks, and makes her mind grow dangerously wild. She fears then she may walk crookedly, may fall absurdly on account of a misstep, or because of that moment's blindness may run blankly into someone who would guess her disturbance.

Carrying these painfully intense visions, Rosaura walks arm in arm with her friends, and plunges into dreadfully flat talk to hide and disguise them.

But the green tranquil light becomes a red, color of blood and passion. Two meters above the rails the monster eye of the locomotive runs flaming brighter, and then passes beyond, as the steely forehead of the engine turns to the horizon. There is the shock of yielding metal. Rosaura suffers, arm in arm with her friends indifferently lost in Sunday laughter.

And one afternoon—strange!—when she sought in the frame of the window that profile which had been to her an intangible, fugitive ideal calling forth dreams, and no more, she saw the man descend with his great suitcase; stride across the crowd on the platform, and take a cab of old Torres, with the gesture of a landlord returning to his estate.

Rosaura felt her soul pierced by the anguish of a virgin possessed.

She was displeased by the active, direct, now-justified teasing of her friends. She left them with scant caresses to flutter the streets with their stale and flat chatter, and fled home in amazement, fearful and dazzled as a quail.

VII.

Rosaura slept badly all that night, pursued by a vague event whose influence would definitely change her life.

Already roused she heard her father in the kitchen, splitting wood for the morning *mate*.

She joined the old man, surprising him with that unnecessary rising.

"Where will the sun come up?"

"It's you, daddy, that woke me."

"Well, go on out to the hen coop and bring in some kindling."

Dawn lighted the yard when Rosaura in quest of the chips saw Lucio's coach ready to leave.

"I'm going to the hotel, *niña*, to get a stranger who's come to look at *haciendas*."

"And why the extra harness?"

"Seems we're goin' to go far . . . maybe 'till tonight."

Lucio twisted his half-open mouth and clapped his tongue on his palate, clucking the horses to start: the uneven team disappeared through the gate, the coach seemed to drop in a hole, comical and shameless as a street wench.

"Good-bye, *niña*!"

The coachman had exaggerated; when Rosaura went down toward the main street that afternoon, after speaking to Doña Petrona, she was struck with surprise upon seeing Carlos seated at a small table in front of the hotel, accompanied by the political leader Barrios, the cattle auctioneer Gonzalez, the representative Iturri and other gentlemen of the hour.

Naturally Carlos bowed to her like the rest and Rosaura answered courteously though she felt naked in her blushes. How hard to maintain a natural walk and how awful to linger like that before ten staring men!

Rosaura's pride suffered and the susceptible little creole, hurt by that supposedly betraying blush, hated the stranger violently. Why couldn't things remain as they were, easy?

78

She was overcome by a fear of having to talk to Carlos in public. She believed her platform flirtation so flagrant.

Oh, indeed! She would make him pay for that humiliation, doubtless already glossed by the clumsy words of that shameless crowd in front of the Hotel de Paris; nobody should have a peg on which to hang a tale about *her* favours.

And that afternoon at the glory hour of Lobos, Rosaura, wounded in the privacy of her romantic passion, became singularly talkative and attentive to the chatter of her friends, returned their shafts charmingly, and cruelly, suicidally ridiculed the elegant youth, who followed her with his eyes fixed steadily as the headlights of an automobile on the road.

When Rosaura went home she was exhausted and convinced that she had been uselessly a coward; she threw herself on the bed and, pathetically disheveled, wept great sobs of pain for her blighted passion.

VIII.

Fortunately that state of affairs did not last. Rosaura would have died of grief. It was not possible to weep so, days and days, accusing herself bitterly.

Carlos had left on the morning following that, to him, incomprehensible afternoon.

No actions proved, and no words even, that the saucy flirtation of the girl the platform meant anything more than a few moments' diversion. Hurt by the impudence of the staring little chit in the yellow dress, he thought no more of the matter, unaware that he left a great passion tortured into a sorrow, as the train jerked from the station in the biting chill of that windy morning.

79

In the garden that smelled of jasmine, honeysuckle and carnations, little Rosaura wilted like a flower bruised by some casual hummingbird which flitted on, once it had sucked the savor.

Ended forever, the gay starts every afternoon at five; the hellos to Doña Petrona; the coquettishly careful crossings; the fastidious resentment at the brutal stares of the loungers in front of the Hotel de Paris, the meetings with her friends and the glorified walks on the platform, before those eyes that kindled and pierced her.

There was nothing left but to weep, weep forever, for these memories of her broken life.

Rosaura would have died had she thought that the fashionable youth of the dining car would never come back, or would pass in the train as indifferent to her as the monster eye of the locomotive to the ideal of the horizon.

It was five. Rosaura recalled even the slightest movements of her habit of years and years. Impatience pulled her to the dressing table, but a presentiment of martyrdom dropped her on her knees before the niche adorned with palms crossed ovally, where her little blue Madonna spangled with gold prayed, in mystic stance, through the centuries.

Oh, that he might be returned to her with a smile of forgiveness; that she might receive only two affectionate lines so as not to die strangled by this thing so much bigger than herself!

Three dry little knocks of somebody's knuckles on the door announced a discreet visitor. Rosaura hurriedly arranged her pitifully disordered self, and in Carmen, the friend of the pink dress who had been deserted so long, in the distress of that wrecked love. And as Rosaura's arms passionately convulsive about her were a confession, Carmen, charmingly comforting, spoke openly:

"Holy Mother, be still! Why, I've a piece of news that will just make you laugh!"

Rosaura, turned to the wall to hide her tears, quivered from head to foot and her shoulders shook with deep, painful sobs.

"Don't cry like that . . . you'd do better to start making a peach of a dress for the dance that the Club is giving next week . . . Or don't you care?"

"Don't joke with me, Carmen."

"Joke? Sit down and listen to real information . . . I know who he is, what he thinks of you, what he came for and a lot of other things."

"And who told you all that?"

"Gonzalez, who showed him the cows for Lorenzo Ramallo."

"And what's he got to do with Ramallo?"

"Nothing much, he's his son, that's all."

From being overcome by that name known far and wide as one of the cream of landholders, Rosaura's passion rose with this new impossibility. So long as Carlos passed thorough on the train, so long as he came now and then to the little village of Lobos, so long as he looked at her as he had, her love would seek more impulses to grow.

"What else did he say?" she murmured tremblingly.

"That you're a marvel and that he's coming to the dance at the Club to meet you. Now cry if you want!"

Rosaura did not weep but she paled unbelievably. She suffered a torment of pleasure and that fulfillment was as painful as a pregnancy.

More than ever the rings deepened under her eyes, beneath her drooped eyelids; and while Carmen ran merrily on, a smile rose to her lips from the calm depths of her love in contemplation.

IX.

Came a tranquil time to the Torres place. The little garden sprouted under the caress of the sun. The orchard bore amply either side of the arboured vine. The red-crested Ceibo Tree scattered fine glints in the shimmering air. The dog chased mischievously around the edges of feminine skirts, balancing the silver notes of whimper like a tune rehearsed in a nightingale's nest.

On the porch enclosed by the fresh bloom of its vines, Rosaura sewed leaning back in her chair. Patches of sunlight dropped on the dress through the vines the leaves overhead; and when with an indolent foot she would start the chair rocking, those imperceptible wavelets of warmth ran carelessly over her body.

At her right a bent-legged sewing basket spread out like a split nut, its contents brimming, and on the left a little table unevenly set on the flags, threatened to drop a fashion review lent by a friend on one of the estates for the occasion of the Club dance.

Happy, the lovely Rosaura, absorbed in her work, threaded promises of her love on the porch shaded by the quiet garden stirred in the spring.

Rosaura had chosen from among the models a pattern of muslin embroidered with buds and sprays of fern fine as cobwebs. It opened a bare timid triangle at the neck and a great sash with a bow on one side fluffed like a full rose.

How much she knew now of the Carlos heretofore so mysterious and so untold! Carlos had been educated in Europe. On his return Don Lorenzo, his father, had given him the place at General Alvear to manage, which, however, did not hinder later travels into countries fabulous
to Rosaura.

What a new wreath of glory all of this laid upon him, in the heart of the romantic little provincial!

She would go with him as in the fairytales, to enchanting and beautiful lands where everything is as easy as dreaming and where to love is to fulfill the most sacred duty. Her hand would be held in his and we would tell her about everything, knowing everything. Then they would return to the little garden, and would live in the neighborhood that reminded them of
other days.

Rosaura ran the needle into her finger. One of the buds on the musling blushed deeper, and she, annoyed at this stupid break in her rhythmic trance, pressed the tip of the hurt finger, making a tiny crimson source.

The dress was finished on time.

X.

The grayish façade of the Club Social occupied twenty yards of the cobblestoned street; from its windows streamed a blaze of festive light, promising gaiety.

At nine that night the hearts of the Lobos girls beat fast, this being the hour to put the last touches on the frocks that would mean scorn or envy. Only

Rosaura, pale as a bride, shivers running over her body in its springtime festoon of sprays and buds, remained indifferent to such petty social successes.

She had arrayed herself with the delicate care of a miniaturist, drawing on long stiff silk hose, finished off by the bright patentleather pumps; her skin quivered at the touch of the fine white undergarment spangled with yellow bows, fitted snugly to her torso by the girdle, rose-faint as a blush. And she had called her mother to gaze as she slipped into the rustling folds of the frock.

It was time. She walked toward the mirror tasting, at the measured swing of her step, the barely tangible subtlety of her airy garments; she walked profiled, as an apparition; smiled faintly, lifting in quick amazement her mobile eyebrows, and she thought she might please because of that shade of docility in her eyes, messengers of miracles.

It was time and she was ready, pure and vibrant as a crystal shivered by the note of a bronze bell. She swooned almost, with virginal ripeness of sacrifice, sensing herself worshipped by the intact garments, adorned with the solemn splendours of an offering. "Oh, yes, all his." And a momentary loss of consciousness sent her swaying for support to the bureau, where her hand, limp and cold, lay like marble on the red glamour of the mahogany.

"Come on, come on! . . ." The door opened filling the room with brief clamour. The Gomez girls had arrived to fetch her, as agreed, and Rosaura folded in on herself, like a sensitive plant.

In the dance hall of the Club Social, revealed inconsiderately by the hard, blinding lights, the reception committee, self-conscious and solemn, fenced opportunely.

Carlos, acquainted with the gloved punctiliousness of such parties, had come early, to settle himself comfortably in a private corner.

An air of naïve cordiality already reigned, and they had all become more used to the gala dress, when the auctioneer Gonzalez waving a hand from left to right, spoke their names softly:

"Señor Carlos Ramallo, señorita Rosaura Torres."

To Rosaura, that coupling of their names attained the significance of a question before the altar.

"Very pleased, señor," she said, and she thought this was everything.

He gave her his arm properly.

"As to me I confess it was almost absolutely necessary to speak to you, since I look upon you as an old friend."

Rosaura blushed:

"It is true, we have seen each other so often."

Oh, the melodious enchantment of walking thus, arm in arm, with their words moving close to confession!

And all Lobos looking on!

"Shall we sit down?"

"If you like."

They went out through the corridor, toward a bench glimpsed in the patio, suddenly glorified by the luminous glitter of stars, in a sky framed by the naïve grey cornice.

"This is nice."

They sat down, relieved of pretense; night knows nothing of etiquette and love is everywhere, naturally.

They were silent. Rosaura, quiet, looking at the button of her glove and in the comradely tone that the night required, queried:

"Tell me about yourself. Would you mind? I have lived so alone here."

Carlos did not reply. To tell the child, simple as a red bloom, of his intricate fashionable adventures would be the irreverent action of a cheap Don Juan.

"Please believe my amusements don't amount to anything."

"But—and all you have traveled in this wide world?"

"I have some pleasant memories."

And carried away in the mood of Rosaura, who intently waited for wondrous tales, he seemed to have just discovered the true charm of things past.

Surprised to hear himself saying sincerely:

"These journeys are saddening when one makes them alone."

With what further absurdities would he continue?

But Rosaura, surmising an indirect allusion, toyed more intently with her glove, purchased for the ball.

Scenting a new fad, other couples followed Carlos and Rosaura toward the patio, and the night, its silence broken, was dethroned. Carlos recalled other scenes trilled too with laughter and dizzied with perfumes.

"Will you dance?"

But another youth claimed that polka from Rosaura. Carlos found himself alone and near his friend the auctioneer, so he begged to be presented to other girls, saying to himself that thus he would mask his reason for coming to the dance.

The daughter of Barrios was a lovely wench of excited voice, from whose pouter-pigeon bosom gushed a tangle of the most astonishing speeches.

What a relief, what a pleasure, when he found himself again with the simple Rosaura, love entire, on a bench in the patio now emptied by the greed that free refreshments awakened!

"Oh, Señorita, how your friends weary me!"

"Don't call me Señorita."

"Thank you, Rosaura, how all these little Sunday girls bore me. If I couldn't feel myself a friend of yours, I would dash out at a gallop. Stay with me a while, as long or as short as you please, and I shall be grateful."

"You see how quickly we understand each other," laughed Rosaura. "But unfortunately I would have to hear tales if I stayed as long as I'd like."

"Would it be very long?"

Rosaura turned again to the button of her glove, and they were silent, overcome by discoveries mutually guessed.

One must, when one cannot speak from the soul, touch on simple things to hear undisturbed the song within.

"Are you always bored, Rosaura?"

"Not before. I had enough with my work and my walks to the station or to the plaza, where I met my friends and we would amuse ourselves with our jokes and our foolishness. Now I want more. The town seems so dreary, and I think of how you travel so much, have seen so many things."

"And yet you see I come here."

To say something, terrified by the consequences of her own words, Rosaura murmured:

87

"You must have a reason."

"Don't you know it?"

"Why should I know it?"

Rosaura was suffering now. Carlos' eyebrows were drawn tightly together, hardening his espression. Something vaguely in his smile prophesied who knows what dreadful phrase.

"Please, Carlos, be still."

The eyebrows were calmed, the forced smile disappeared:

"We do not need to say much."

It was true, and as the fraternally-begun conversation had turned difficult, Carlos again told stories of his restless life to the little provincial so childishly attuned with her trustful eyes.

This intimate chat bridged a long time easily, and then Carlos with the air of a guardian said:

"Well, go and dance now with your friends, or they'll be saying that we are sweethearts."

"Oh, heavens!"

"Anyhow we are good friends."

"Yes, but now, who knows when you'll come back."

"You'll see . . . I have it arranged so that it won't be so seldom."

Rosaura went back to the hall, leaving Carlos without thinking to ask him to explain.

And thus ended the first meeting of the provincial girl with the elegant youth of the diner, now a cordial friend: which is not little for an ideal that passes, rousing great dreams that can never come true.

88

XI.

From then on, after that night so brimful of lover's portent, the six-thirty-five express no longer carried an intangible ideal, the youth of the diner in his frame of light. Carlos had found a better solution and sacrificing the sluggishness of a bad sleeper, took the train at five in the morning to spend the day in Lobos.

The pretexts, though weak, would suffice: To see his friend the auctioneer Gonzalez, to go uselessly to his sales, or simply to shorten the six monotonous hours of the usual journey.

What are pretexts when two lives are drawn to each other?

The sun was high when Carlos descended hampered by his London suitcase checkered with hotel labels.

Scarcely anybody stood on the platform, so crowded in the half-hour between the two express trains, the six o'clock and the six-thirty-five. One of old Torres' cabs took him to the Hotel de Paris where he "made the morning" with Gonzalez, Iturri, and other personages of the hour. He lunched with the appetite of a traveler and slept a restful siesta till four, when he took tea facing the cobblestoned street which fluttered already in prospect of the daily promenade.

All this just for the little half hour in the afternoon, in the teeming confusion of the crowded platform: politicians out on campaign, young men in gray felts and light shoes, personages displaying their official personalities, sheiks with straw hats about to slide off their greasy foreheads and stickily pomaded skulls, coachmen waiting for fares, peons for mail or on errands. While like aromatic blooms in a virgin forest, the Lobos girls passed flirtatious and mocking.

From end to end of the platform, flanked by her friends, the one in pink and the one in sky blue, Rosaura walked with the tread of a coquette, returning the glances of Carlos, her affectionate friends with smiles that opened like flowers.

And Carlos filled his eyes with that dainty loved figure which retreated as if in anger, or gazed into those docile pupils open and penetrable as windows wide to a tryst.

But the cars of the express clanked unevenly in. The asthmatic gasps of the locomotive died down.

The blazing train drew up in front of the covered station and shut out the night.

People ascended, people descended, the minutes scrambled down the restless clock; on the dusty haunch of the diner, while speaking her last shy words farewell, Rosaura traced the initials of an idyll. And suddenly, tearing a great wound through the soul of the little enamoured provincial, a brutal screech announced the departure. The cars flew apart like the vertebrae of a reptile in flight; the iron of joints and bumpers clanged from locomotive to caboose. Carlos bowed, quickly smaller at a sudden distance. The caboose passed rapidly, striking from the station windows a vibrant near echo.

And before Rosaura rose the deep indifference of the spangled night, painfully stifling the fugitive blare of the train which flies with the blind gaze of its monster eye toward the horizon whose attraction it does not comprehend.

Poor little Rosaura, abandoned thus to that passion too large for herself, in the deadly boredom of the village lost in a pampa that ignores the way of romance in its children.

XII.

Nevertheless, except for the disconsolate parting that wounded as if it were forever, Rosaura's life overflowed happiness.

In her garden now heightened beyond springtime budding, the lilac dropped fragrant sprays and the fresh porch flourished green, spattered with morning glories, jasmines and honeysuckle.

Yielding to the soft breath of summer, Rosaura dreamed warmly through the stream of hours.

Seated in her rocking chair, bathed in the odor of flowers, she works without ceasing, the needle quick in her skilled hands.

At her right, the sewing basket on its bent legs spreads open like a split nut, contents brimming. To her left, a little table unevenly set on the flags holds scattered colourful fashion books borrowed from that friend who had sent her the first for the dance at the Club Social.

Happy beyond explanation, the little Rosaura intent on her work lives with memories of meetings with her beloved Carlos so worthy of all the passions.

Rosaura had many patterns because she had quickly found herself deplorably provincial in her country clothing. And what feminine delight to devote all her days thus to sheathing herself in chaste caressing undergarments. Oh, the bows and the weaves white as holy wafers around her virgin body, all an offering to the mysterious rites of adoration! Gentle murmurs of future bliss steal into dreams. She would be worthy of him, simple and naïve but still passionate and tender in the radiant fire of a love all immolation.

Elusively identical the days passed in the little garden of the Torres stables, idealized by the intense soul of Rosaura, always certain that her Carlos would come tomorrow, day after tomorrow, or next week, to tell her with his eyes that he loved her, put in her hand a nosegay of strange country blossoms, and in the afternoon to take a departure as painful as if forever, but to return because that was fate.

XIII.

Night knowing something of sorcery transformed the insipid plaza of the town. Night, the blue, the stars; reducing the visible world to a few pools of light wept the lamps, immobile, isolate and sad, condemned to stay forever, although they aspire desperately td be stars: a desire aroused by the springtime infinity of the depthless sky.

The people, limited to their bodies, tread the slavery of the plaza paths made to walk on, and cannot escape in perishable desires.

And so their souls into fling themselves into impossible futures and migrate from love to love, as does light from star to star, drilling through the spaces that bar the victory of matter.

But it is the same plaza. The bushes and hedges clipped like thick manes shape greenish-black geometric figures curiously similar to human forms. The paths curve, lacking space in which to be true roads that know where they are going. A few trees, newly green, have become thus tender in response to the benison of spring on time as always.

The groups of girls are like displays under glass of souls that will love, and the men long impossibly to clasp a bunch of them with feverish hands.

Carlos comes when he can to this holiday parade on the plaza stretched out under the stars, beneath the holy watch of the colonial bell tower, where with infinite forgiveness God blesses his straying sentimental lambs.

In that luminous scene of fans, skirts and blouses, the most beautiful is Rosaura and also the farthest from herself; for she is carried off by great dreams of a heroine of romance, pining for the hero who has appeared from an unbelievable land, with a halo of the glamorous unknown.

Oh! . . . to be thus chosen among all!

Night, that knows something of sorcery, filters its temptation into the hearts of those people, who, God be thanked,, have their morals; that is why this does not end here, with the most natural of love's solutions.

XIV.

Thus Rosaura reached the height of her glory. Carlos' intervals of absence were brief, in which to savour every word, every gesture; and their meetings were fulfillments whose intuitive comprehensions made vows superfluous; rapture floated around them, as if exhaled by their emotions.

But that state of their souls perhaps called disaster upon them, as lightning by the crosses that pray on cupolas.

Carlos, pretending to take the matter lightly, told her he was leaving shortly for Europe:

". . . Oh! For a very short time; three or four months at the most . . . through the summer. . . . I can't avoid it; my father would be very much surprised and he might even be angry. . . ."

Rosaura, mortally wounded, listened with anguish.

"Tell me, Carlos. Isn't Señor Ramallo sending you away?"

"What an idea, child! And why should he?"

"Don't know . . . maybe they've told him that you're wasting your time in some little village."

"No, Rosaura, what a notion!"

Carlos explained again. Who would know and if they did, who would think think bad of his visits to Lobos? But it meant much to his father for him to make this trip to England, where he would learn a great deal studying the best-known model farms under a competent person.

"Three or four months . . . it seems so long, Carlos!"

He answered her, for the first time with a plain meaning:

"Rosaura, believe me, even if I were gone six, they would be too few to erase certain things."

"Sure?"

"Very sure."

Life sprang again in the little village girl. Carlos spoke with so much assurance that his absence seemed more bearable, and the especially tender pitch of that beloved voice was deceptive balm to her sensitive soul. Furthermore, Rosaura possessed the greatness of noble trust, and an extraordinary feminine delight in sacrificing herself to the will of her idol. In her eyes Carlos could do nothing wrong. And that poor night they parted; their hands more than ever revealed their love, despite all human obstacles.

XV.

It was summer, and of Carlos nothing remained in Lobos except the increasing passion of his Rosaura and a brief note of farewell in her hands.

Life went on as usual in the Torres household, except for the lengthened burdensome days, the greater fatigue of the horses and the always perspiring peons, the sleepy inertia of the throbbing siesta hour, and the sadness of the poor girl, drooping now like a flower prostrated by the full blaze of the sun.

Nevertheless, her faith firm in her Carlos, Rosaura laboured to embellish herself. Her provincial wardrobe disappeared totally and no one, by her clothing, would have distinguished the former showy little country girl in yellow from a fashionable urban young lady.

This clothing that wove its knowing charms around her was born of the wish to seem elegant to him, and its contact filled, though imperfectly, the void left by the want of other caresses.

How daring dreams are; and how, by sheer familiarity with her more and more definite vision of what might happen, Rosaura grew to feel that she had been incredibly timid.

She did not know how, but she was certain that on Carlos' return their love would take a more natural course, and this prodded her anxious count of the long days.

But time passed with all its apparent slowness, while Rosaura worked to make herself beautiful, cared for her person as for an idol that belonged to someone else, and for whose pricelessness she was responsible. At this stage she never doubted the love of her Carlos.

XVI.

Incurable sadness floated in the little garden of the Torres place, breathed off by the approaching winter that blighted the flowers so merrily brought by the spring.

The autumn petals were seared by the cold, the last stunted peaches dropped from their boughs, the arbour was stripped of its grapes and the little garden so piteously rifled bore a seal of arid harshness.

A mild patch of sunlight filtered on the porch, overhung by once matted vines, gilding the withered leaves. Rosaura, pale with her first woman's sorrow, had lost her youthful jasmine smoothness and her honeysuckle lushness; and abetted by sleepless outpourings of tears, the violet rings under her eyes triumphantly deepened to the transparent sheen of grapes.

Poor little Rosaura, tender aimless fancy; the fragrance of whose love was worthy of immortalizing a whole town's prosaic staleness.

Poor little Rosaura, victim of a moment of fateful evolution; incurable longing of simple things for the meshes of splendor; on her simple faith in the promise of a beyond, turned all her disaster.

Her fate was to suffer and no other, because thus says a homely proverb: "Who looks too far upward may break his neck."

Her grief was as fatal as the race of melting snow downward.

Immensely sad is the little garden of the Torres place. From the soul small of its small mistress disconsolate dreams ebb, while autumn falls like a shroud upon that corner of the world, lost in the middle of the changeless pampa that knows nothing of romantic loves.

## XVII.

A nervous anxiety aroused Rosaura from the dejection in which she lived. Carlos might come any moment.

The daughter of Crescencio Torres returned to her old habits and except for Carmen or whoever in the village possessed the gift of divination, Lobos ignored the change in the spirit of its lovely child.

About five-thirty Rosaura went out in an airy blouse, cut triangularly at the neck, dark blue skirt, and calf pumps, though bareheaded so as not to be too conspicuous among her friends. Half a block down she stopped to speak to old Petrona unweariedly standing on the threshold of her white house, her arms pillowed on the soft mound of her stomach shaken with deep laughter.

"Hello, Doña Petrona."

"God bless you, child . . . my, the poor boys, you're a regular poster . . . Holy Mary! Why you're right up to the minute!

But Rosaura would not hear.

On the main street, fashionable Lobos promenaded, fluttering with chatter the paths shaded by hoary elms.

Afternoon would be winding itself out in the corners when they gradually invaded the crowded platform.

What an unbearable emotion, this waiting; what torment and overcoming reminder arose in Rosaura at the gleam of the headlight of the locomotive on the rails!

Yes, he will come this afternoon. She will spy him in his window, meeting brilliant joy in his eyes. Her soul will divine his presence and all her old delight will burst forth like a radiant dawn.

"Oh, to fall in his arms!"

But in the glaring frame of that window which once gave life, no face appeared.

XVIII.

The leaves fell, the first chill crept out, and Rosaura suffered like the red autumn blooms that freeze in the flight of the sun.

Was all that romance an illusion?

The poor girl almost believed so, with the daily disappointment of the vacant space in the window of the diner.

But it was not an illusion, because one afternoon when her heart was breaking, Carmen took her by the arm and trembling at the enormity of her announcement said:

"Come here, child, come, I've seen him in another car."

Oh, Rosaura! How to keep a scream from escaping? Her legs refused to advance, though her friend dragged her by the arm. It was true. He was there.

Carlos! . . . Oh, to fall on his beloved breast and to tell him that she never doubted his return, and then so many, many things more! She recognized him through a dim window. Nearly swooning, and almost stretching out her arms, before them all, her upper lip rose smiling faintly; and he bowed merely, as if there had never existed between them anything beyond a passing word.

XIX.

Rosaura fell into a coma of intense pain. Everybody in the house knew that something unusual had happened to her and the mother learned of the drama on the delirious night that followed the incident unperceived by others.

The love of Rosaura, rooted in her like an organism inseparable from her own, was killing her with its death.

Carmen, the friend who had once brought the first-fruits of her love; brought her the gravestone as well:

"Listen, child . . . it isn't worthwhile, suffering for that wicked man!"

"Please, Carmen, let's not speak of it any more."

"It's that I wanted to tell you . . . if you want to notice next time he passes, you'll see that he is with another woman, all dressed up in those things that you like."

"For God's sake be still, Carmen."

So she swallowed the details which her friend brought to be close to her; her lips quivering childishly but with her eyes dry, she burst into sobs long and painful as if her very bowels were being dragged from her slowly.

XX.

Rosaura has come to the station, in her frock of flowered muslin, reminder of that unforgettable night in the Club Social. She has tucked the brief note, the only one from Carlos, in her bosom, the note of farewell, and her convulsive hands crumble to dust the dry petals of the flowers she had kept because he had given them to her.

Rosaura must be a little mad to come dressed like that to the platform. But what does she care what they say?

Carmen is with her, caring for her like a nurse, troubled by those strange fancies, and dressed as always in pink, not having suffered, like her friend, the intense influence of outside things.

Suddenly, Rosaura's hand sinks into the soft flesh of her friend's arm.

"Come on, Carmen, come on for God's sake, I can't stand any more."

Thus together they walked to the end of the platform Carlos (oh, horrible unconsciousness!) rides in a compartment with the unknown woman, and Rosaura does not want to see him.

"Oh, I can't bear any more, I can't bear any more . . . and leave me now, I beg you for the sake of what you love most . . . leave me and go back with the rest, I'm going home."

"But, child, you don't want me to leave you, and you in that state and crying like a lost soul?"

"Yes, for the sake of what you love most, leave me."

What powerful influence made Carmen obey?

The shrill locomotive announced departure. Carmen goes back to the station.

There is a shock of steel, the locomotive snorts its great poisonous crests out upon Lobos, gasping a strenuous start. The train will continue its journey unknown to unknown, from horizon to horizon.

Then the little Rosaura, overcome by a terrible madness, screams, grinding incomprehensible phrases between her teeth that clamp convulsively with pain. And like a springtime butterfly she flashes out, running between the parallel infinities of the rails, her arms forward in useless offering, calling the name of Carlos, for whom it is passionate joy to die, on the road that takes him away, far from her forever.

"Carlos! . . . Carlos! . . ."

The steely din nears her. The swift victory of the train knows nothing of the cries of a passion that knew how to die.

"Carlos! . . ."

And like a snowy feather, the dainty figure in flowered muslin yields to the march of the gigantic locomotive, for whose monster eye the horizon holds no ideal.

# CHAPTER 6: NEW ACTORS ON AN OLD STAGE

There were two main groups of new actors on the stage in Latin America: One was the United States, which began to emerge as an imperial power, especially after intervening in Cuba's War of Independence. The other group comprised the new middle sectors in Latin America, a rising middle class with nationalist tendencies, and a militant working class. Here we see examples of all three actors.

First is José Martí (1853-1895), to whom Cubans refer as the apostle of Cuban independence. He founded the Cuban Revolutionary Party in 1892 to struggle for independence from Spain. Living in exile in the United States—in the belly of the beast, as he put it—he warned Cubans in this 1891 essay not to emulate foreign solutions to their problems but to look to their own creativity. Martí was killed fighting for Cuban independence in 1895.

Martí was prescient about U.S. interests, which were clearly summed up in the Platt Amendment. In 1901, U.S. Sen. Orville Platt drafted the amendment to be attached to the new Cuban constitution; without the amendment, the United States would not remove its occupying forces from the island. The amendment remained a part of the Cuban constitution until 1933.

As industrialization and immigration increased, so did organizing by anarchists and socialists. In this article from the newspaper *Terra Livre*, three anarchist women chide their sister seamstresses for not taking part in general strikes. They reflect not just worker activism but new feminist action as well.

### José Martí: Our America

To govern well requires an understanding and appreciation of local realities. Anyone who would govern well in the Americas does not need to know how the Germans or the French govern themselves, but rather needs to possess a basic knowledge of his own country, its resources, advantages, and problems and how to utilize them for the benefit of the nation, and needs to know local customs and institutions. The goal is to reach that happy state in which everyone can enjoy the abundance Nature has bestowed so generously on the Americas. Each must work for that enjoyment and be prepared to defend that abundance with his life. Good government arises from the conditions and needs of each nation. The very spirit infusing government must reflect local realities. Good government is nothing more and nothing less than a balance of local needs and resources.

The person who knows his own environment is far superior to anyone dependent on imported books for knowledge. Such a natural person has more to contribute to society than someone versed in artificial knowledge. The native of mixed ancestry is superior to the white person born here but attracted to foreign ideas. No struggle exists between civilization and barbarism but rather between false erudition and natural knowledge. Natural people are good; they respect and reward wisdom as long as it is not used to degrade, humiliate, or belittle them. They are ready to defend themselves and to demand respect from anyone wounding their pride or threatening their well-being. Tyrants have risen to power by conforming to these natural elements; they also have fallen by betraying them. Our republics have paid through tyranny for their inability to

103

understand the true national reality, to derive from it the best form of government, and to govern accordingly. In a new nation, to govern is to create.

In nations inhabited by both the educated and the uneducated, the uneducated will govern because it is their nature to confront and resolve problems with their hands, while the educated dither over which formula to import, a futile means to resolve local problems. The uneducated people are lazy and timid in matters related to intelligence and seek to be governed well, but if they perceive the government to be injurious to their interests they will overthrow it to govern themselves. How can our universities prepare men to govern when not one of them teaches anything either about the art of government or the local conditions? The young emerge from our universities indoctrinated with Yankee or French ideas, aspiring to govern a people they do not understand. Those without a rudimentary knowledge of political reality should be barred from a public career. Prizes should be awarded not for the best poetry but for the best essays on national reality. Journalists, professors, and academicians ought to be promoting the study of national reality. Who are we, where have we been, which direction should we go? It is essential to ask such basic questions in our search for truth. To fail to ask the right questions or to fail to answer them truthfully dooms us. We must know the problems in order to respond to them, and we must know our potentials in order to realistically frame our responses. Strong and indignant natural people resent the imposition of foreign solutions, the insidious result of sterile book learning, because they have little or nothing to do with local conditions and realities. To know those realities is to possess the potential to resolve problems. To know our counters and to govern them in accordance with that knowledge is the only way to liberate ourselves from tyranny. Europeanized education here must give way to American education. The history of the Americas, from the Incas to the present, must be taught in detail even if we forego the courses on ancient Greece. Our own Greece is much more preferable to the Greece which is not ours. It is more important and meaningful to us. Statesmen with a nationalist view must replace politicians whose heads are in Europe even thought their feet remain in the Americas. Graft the world onto our nations if you will, but the trunk itself must be us. Silence the pedant who thrives on foreign inspiration.

There are no lands in which a person can take a greater pride than in our own long-suffering American republics. The Americas began to suffer, and still suffer, from the effort of trying to reconcile the discordant and hostile elements which they inherited from a despotic and greedy colonizer. Imported ideas and institutions with scant relationship to local realities have retarded the development of logical and useful governments. Our continent, disoriented for three centuries by governance that denied people the right to exercise reason, began in independence by ignoring the humble who had contributed so much in the effort to redeem it. At least in theory, reason was to reign in all things and for everyone, not just scholastic reason at the expense of the simpler reason of the majority. But the problem with our independence is that we changed political formulas without altering our colonial spirit.

The privileged made common cause with the oppressed to terminate a system which they found opposed to their own best interests. The colonies continue to survive in the guise of republics. Our America struggles to save itself from the monstrous errors of the past—its haughty capital cities, the blind triumph over the disdained masses, the excessive reliance on foreign ideas, and unjust, impolitic hatred of the native races—and relies on innate virtues and sacrifices to replace our colonial mentality with that of free peoples.

With our chest of an athlete, our hands of a gentleman, and our brain of a child, we presented quite a sight. We masqueraded in English breeches, a French vest, a Yankee jacket, and a Spanish hat. The silent Indians hovered near us but took their children into the mountains to orient them. The Afro-Americans, isolated in this continent, gave expression to thought and sorrow through song. The peasants, the real creators, viewed with indignation the haughty cities. And we the intellectuals wore our fancy caps and gowns in countries where the population dressed in headbands and sandals. Our genius will be in the ability to combine headband and cap, to amalgamate the cultures of the European, Indian, and Afro-American, and to ensure that all who fought for liberty enjoy it. Our colonial past left us with judges, generals, scholars, and bureaucrats. The idealistic young have been frustrated in efforts to bring change. The people have been unable to translate triumph into benefits. The European and Yankee books hold no answers for our problems and our future. Our problems grow. Frustrations mount. Exhausted by these problems and frustrations, by the struggles between the intellectual and the military, between reason and superstition, between the city and the countryside, and by the contentious urban politicians who abuse the natural nation, tempestuous or inert by turns, we turn now to a new compassion and understanding.

The new nations look about, acknowledging each other. They ask, "Who and what are we?" We suggest tentative answers. When a local problem arises, we are less likely to seek the answer in London or Paris. Our styles may all still originate in France but our thought is becoming more American. The

106

new generation rolls up its sleeves, gets its hands dirty, and sweats. It is getting results. Our youth now understands that we are too prone to imitate and that our salvation lies in creativity. "Creativity" is the password of this new generation. The wine is from the plantain, and even if it is bitter, it is our wine! They understand that the form a government takes in a given country must reflect the realities of that country. Fixed ideas must become relative in order for them to work. Freedom to experiment must be honest and complete. If these republics do not include all their populations and benefit all of them, then they will fail.

The new American peoples have arisen; they look about; they greet each other. A new leadership emerges which understands local realities. New leaders read and study in order to apply their new knowledge, to adapt it to local realities, not to imitate. Economists study problems with an historical context. Orators eschew flamboyance for sober reality. Playwrights people the stages with local characters. Academicians eschew scholastic theories to discuss pressing problems. Poets eschew marble temples and Gothic cathedrals in favor of local scenes. Prose offers ideas and solutions. In those nations with large Indian populations, the Presidents are learning to speak Indian languages.

The greatest need of Our America is to unite in spirit. The scorn of our strong neighbor the United States is the greatest present danger to Our America. The United States now pays greater attention to us. It is imperative that this formidable neighbor get to know us in order to dissipate its scorn. Through ignorance, it might even invade and occupy us. Greater knowledge of us will increase our neighbor's understanding and diminish that threat.

A new generation reshapes our continent. This new generation recreates Our America. It sows the seeds of a New America from the Río

107

Grande to the Straits of Magellan. The hopes of Our America lie in the originality of the new generation.

Source: Text adapted from "Nuestra America," *El Partido Liberal* (Mexico City), January 30, 1891, p. 4, by E. Bradford Burns, ed., *Latin America: Conflict and Creation, A Historical Reader* (Englewood Cliffs, NJ: Prentice Hall, 1993), 110-113.

# Platt Amendment

Whereas the Congress of the United States of America, by an Act approved March 2, 1901, provided as follows:

Provided further, That in fulfillment of the declaration contained in the joint resolution approved April twentieth, eighteen hundred and ninety-eight, entitled "For the recognition of the independence of the people of Cuba, demanding that the Government of Spain relinquish its authority and government in the island of Cuba, and withdraw its land and naval forces from Cuba and Cuban waters, and directing the President of the United States to use the land and naval forces of the United States to carry these resolutions into effect," the President is hereby authorized to "leave the government and control of the island of Cuba to its people" so soon as a government shall have been established in said island under a constitution which, either as a part thereof or in an ordinance appended thereto, shall define the future relations of the United States with Cuba, substantially as follows:

"I. That the government of Cuba shall never enter into any treaty or other compact with any foreign power or powers which will impair or tend to impair the independence of Cuba, nor in any manner authorize or permit any foreign power or powers to obtain by colonization or for military or naval purposes or otherwise, lodgement in or control over any portion of said island."

"II. That said government shall not assume or contract any public debt, to pay the interest upon which, and to make reasonable sinking fund provision for the ultimate discharge of which, the ordinary revenues of the island, after defraying the current expenses of government shall be inadequate."

"III. That the government of Cuba consents that the United States may exercise the right to intervene for the preservation of Cuban independence, the maintenance of a government adequate for the protection of life, property, and individual liberty, and for discharging the obligations with respect to Cuba imposed by the treaty of Paris on the United States, now to be assumed and undertaken by the government of Cuba."

"IV. That all Acts of the United States in Cuba during its military occupancy thereof are ratified and validated, and all lawful rights acquired thereunder shall be maintained and protected."

"V. That the government of Cuba will execute, and as far as necessary extend, the plans already devised or other plans to be mutually agreed upon, for the sanitation of the cities of the island, to the end that a recurrence of epidemic and infectious diseases may be prevented, thereby assuring protection to the people and commerce of Cuba, as well as to the commerce of the southern ports of the United States and the people residing therein."

"VI. That the Isle of Pines shall be omitted from the proposed constitutional boundaries of Cuba, the title thereto being left to future adjustment by treaty."

"VII. That to enable the United States to maintain the independence of Cuba, and to protect the people thereof, as well as for its own defense, the government of Cuba will sell or lease to the United States lands necessary for coaling or naval stations at certain specified points to be agreed upon with the President of the United States."

"VIII. That by way of further assurance the government of Cuba will embody the foregoing provisions in a permanent treaty with the United States."

Source: "The Platt Amendment," in *Treaties and Other International Agreements of the United States of America, 1776-1949*, vol. 8, ed. C.I. Bevans (Washington, D.C.: United States Government Printing Office, 197 1), pp. 1116-17. Historical Text Archive © 2003

## Anarchist Women in São Paulo

COMRADES!

Because of the apathy dominating you which you have not yet shaken off, even in this city where we are so exploited, we resolve to make a new attempt to defend all of us. We hope you will not allow us to remain the only ones demanding our indisputable rights. In all fairness, you should recall that many times some friends have come to our defense in the newspaper columns of *Avanti!*, *La Battaglia*, and *Terra Livre*. But their words were not heard. We hope you will not abandon us also to cry out alone in this wilderness.

We must finally demonstrate that we are capable of demanding our due. If we maintain our solidarity, if you fight with us, if are heard, we shall begin by exposing the greed of the blood-sucking employers.

The last general strike in this city clearly proved that the seamstresses are the most ignorant and backward group among the working classes. In that movement of worker solidarity, all the skilled workers participated, from the mechanics to the cabinet makers, from the iron workers to the carpenters, plus hat workers, masons, carriage makers, almost all the printers, factory workers in textile, clothing, and match plants, marble cutters, goldsmiths, and many others. In Jundiaí retail commerce made common cause with the strikers by shutting their doors. Here in São Paulo students demonstrated their sympathy and the law school had to be closed. And we, the seamstresses, what did we do?

We remained apathetic and unconcerned while strikers filled the city streets. We still went to our .jobs, thereby showing that we had no feelings, that we had no blood in our veins. In the mass of strikers were our fathers, our brothers, our sweethearts, and we walked among them without realizing that they were demanding our rights also. Thus we demonstrated our lack of family affection and love!

Reflect, comrades, that we too must always maintain our solidarity with those struggling for the liberation of labor if we wish any aid from others in achieving our more than
just demands.

Comrades! It is essential that we refuse to work night and day because that is disgraceful and inhuman. Since 1856 men in many places have attained the eight hour day. But we members of the weaker sex have to work up to sixteen hours a day, double that of the stronger sex! Comrades, think about your futures; if you continue to allow yourselves to be weakened and the last drop of your blood drained off, then, after you have lost your physical energy, motherhood will be martyrdom and your children will be pale and sickly.

You should speak about these matters not only with your families, but also with our inhuman employers, face to face. After all, their businesses grow and prosper day by day. Go at night to protest and give these thieves a caning if necessary! Come, without delay and energetically pull out the claws of those greedy exploiters! Do you have much to lose? What do they give us—those vulture—in payment for our toil? A ridiculous salary. A miserable pittance!

We too would like to have leisure time to read or study, for we have little education. If the current situation continues, through our lack of consciousness, we shall always be mere human machines manipulated at will by she greediest assassins and thieves.

How can anyone read a book if he or she leaves for work at seven o'clock in the morning and returns home at eleven o'clock at night? We have only eight hours left out of every twenty-four, insufficient time to recuperate our strength and to overcome our exhaustion through sleep! We have no future. Our horizons are bleak. We are born to be exploited and to die in ignorance like animals.

We hope you will not abandon us, comrades, and that you will aid us to lay bare and oppose the employers' infamous outrages that must be ended. Yes! We count on the support of our sisters and comrades. The victory will be ours. Let us get to work!

Tecla Fabbri, Teresa Cari, Maria Lopes


Source: *Terra Livre*, July 29, 1906, p. 2, reprinted in *Women in Latin American History: their lives and views,* June E. Hahner, ed. Los Angeles: UCLA Latin American Center Publications, 1980, 116-118.

# CHAPTER 7: THE MEXICAN REVOLUTION

The Mexican Revolution began with Francisco Madero's call to arms against Porfirio Díaz in 1910. But Madero, a wealthy rancher, wanted political revolution, not a social and economic one. He was challenged by Emiliano Zapata's call for Land and Liberty. The views of each leader can be seen in their respective plans: Madero's Plan de San Luis Potosí, and Zapata's Plan de Ayala.

The voice of the common soldier in the revolution could be heard in the *corridos* that they sang, and none was more famous than *La Adelita*. The song celebrates the Mexican *soldadera*, women who were not just camp followers who cooked and sewed for their men, but who picked up guns and fought as soldiers.

## Madero's Plan de San Luís Potosí

Peoples, in their constant efforts for the triumph of the ideal of liberty and justice, are forced, at precise historical moments, to make their greatest sacrifices.

Our beloved country has reached one of those moments. A force of tyranny which we Mexicans were not accustomed to suffer after we won our independence oppresses us in such a manner that it has become intolerable. In exchange for that tyranny we are offered peace, but peace full of shame for the Mexican nation, because its basis is not law, but force; because its object is not the aggrandizement and prosperity of the country, but to enrich a small group who, abusing their influence, have converted the public charges into fountains of exclusively personal benefit, unscrupulously exploiting the manner of lucrative concessions and contracts.

115

The legislative and judicial powers are completely subordinated to the executive; the division of powers, the sovereignty of the States, the liberty of the common councils, and the rights of the citizens exist only in writing in our great charter; but, as a fact, it may almost be said that martial law constantly exists in Mexico; the administration of justice, instead of imparting protection to the weak, merely serves to legalize the plunderings committed by the strong; the judges instead of being the representatives of justice, are the agents of the executive, whose interests they faithfully serve; the chambers of the union have no other will than that of the dictator; the governors of the States are designated by him and they in their turn designate and impose in like manner the municipal authorities.

From this it results that the whole administrative, judicial, and legislative machinery obeys a single will, the caprice of General Porfirio Diaz, who during his long administration has shown that the principal motive that guides him is to maintain himself in power and at any cost.

For many years profound discontent has been felt throughout the Republic, due to such a system of government, but General Diaz with great cunning and perseverance, has succeeded in annihilating all independent elements, so that it was not possible to organize any sort of movement to take from him the power of which he made such bad use. The evil constantly became worse, and the decided eagerness of General Diaz to impose a successor upon the nations in the person of Mr. Ramon Corral carried that evil to its limit and caused many of us Mexicans, although lacking recognized political standing, since it had been impossible to acquire it during the 36 years of dictatorship, to throw ourselves into the struggle to recover the sovereignty of the people and their rights on purely democratic grounds.

In Mexico, as a democratic Republic, the public power can have no other origin nor other basis than the will of the people, and the latter can not be subordinated to formulas to be executed in a fraudulent manner.

For this reason the Mexican people have protested against the illegality of the last election and, desiring to use successively all the recourses offered by the laws of the Republic, in due form asked for the nullification of the election by the Chamber of Deputies, notwithstanding they recognized no legal origin in said body and knew beforehand that, as its members were not the representatives of the people, they would carry out the will of General Diaz, to whom exclusively they owe their investiture.

In such a state of affairs the people, who are the only sovereign, also protested energetically against the election in imposing manifestations in different parts of the Republic; and if the latter were not general throughout the national territory, it was due to the terrible pressure exercised by the Government, which always quenches in blood any democratic manifestation, as happened in Puebla, Vera Cruz, Tlaxcala, and in other places.

But this violent and illegal system can no longer subsist.

I have very well realized that if the people have designated me as their candidate for the Presidency, it is not because they have had an opportunity to discover in me the qualities of a statesman or of a ruler, but the virility of the patriot determined to sacrifice himself, if need be, to obtain liberty and to help the people free themselves from the odious tyranny that oppresses them.

From the moment I threw myself into the democratic struggle I very well knew that General Diaz would not bow to the will of the nation, and the noble Mexican people, in following me to the polls, also knew perfectly the outrage that awaited them; but in spite of it, the people gave the cause of liberty a numerous contingent of martyrs when they were necessary and with wonderful stoicism went to the polls and received every sort of molestation.

But such conduct was indispensable to show to the whole world that the Mexican people are fit for democracy, that they are thirsty for liberty, and that their present rulers do not measure up to their aspirations.

Besides, the attitude of the people before and during the election, as well as afterwards, shows clearly that they reject with energy the Government of General Diaz and that, if those electoral rights had been respected, I would have been elected for President of the Republic.

Therefore, and in echo of the national will, I declare the late election illegal and, the Republic being accordingly without rulers, provisionally assume the Presidency of the Republic until the people designate their rulers pursuant to the law. In order to attain this end, it is necessary to eject from power the audacious usurpers whose only title of legality involves a scandalous and immoral fraud.

With all honesty I declare that it would be a weakness on my part and treason to the people, who have placed their confidence in me, to not put myself at the front of my fellow citizens, who anxiously call me from all parts of the country, to compel General Diaz by force of arms, to respect the national will.

Source: United States Congress, Senate Subcommittee on Foreign Relations, *Revolutions in Mexico*, 62nd Congress, 2nd Session (Washington, D.C.: Government Printing Office, 1913), pp. 730-736, passim. *Internet Modern History Sourcebook*, http://www.fordham.edu.

## Zapata's Plan de Ayala

Liberating Plan of the sons of the State of Morelos, affiliated with the Insurgent Army which defends the fulfillment of the Plan of San Luis, with the reforms which it has believed proper to add in benefit of the Mexican Fatherland.

We who undersign, constituted in a revolutionary junta to sustain and carry out the promises which the revolution of November 20, 1910 just past, made to the country, declare solemnly before the face of the civilized world which judges us and before the nation to which we belong and which we call [*sic, llamamos,* misprint for *amamos,* love], propositions which we have formulated to end the tyranny which oppresses us and redeem the fatherland from the dictatorships which are imposed on us, which [propositions] are determined in the following plan:

I. Taking into consideration that the Mexican people led by Don Francisco I. Madero went to shed their blood to reconquer liberties and recover their rights which had been trampled on, and not for a man to take possession of power, violating the sacred principles which he took an oath to defend under the slogan "Effective Suffrage and No Reelection," outraging thus the faith, the cause, the justice, and the liberties of the people: taking into consideration that that man to whom we refer is Don Francisco I. Madero, the same who initiated the above-cited revolution, who imposed his will and influence as a governing norm on the Provisional Government of the ex-President of the Republic Attorney Francisco L. de Barra [*sic*], causing with this deed repeated sheddings of blood and multiplicate misfortunes for the fatherland in a manner deceitful and ridiculous, having no intentions other than satisfying his personal ambitions, his boundless instincts as a tyrant, and his profound disrespect for the fulfillment of the preexisting laws emanating from the immortal code of '57, written with the revolutionary blood of Ayutla;

Taking into account that the so-called Chief of the Liberating Revolution of Mexico, Don Francisco I. Madero, through lack of integrity and the highest weakness, did not carry to a happy end the revolution which gloriously he initiated with the help of God and the people, since he left standing most of the governing powers and corrupted elements of oppression of the dictatorial government of Porfirio Díaz, which are not nor can in any way be the representation of National Sovereignty, and which, for being most bitter adversaries of ours and of the principles which even now we defend, are provoking the discomfort of the country and opening new wounds in the bosom of the fatherland, to give it its own blood to drink; taking also into account that the aforementioned Sr. Francisco I. Madero, present President of the Republic, tries to avoid the fulfillment of the promises which he made to the Nation in the Plan of San Luis Potosí, being [*sic, siendo*, misprint for *ciñendo*, restricting] the above-cited promises to the agreements of Ciudad Juárez, by means of false promises and numerous intrigues against the Nation nullifying, pursuing, jailing, or killing revolutionary elements who helped him to occupy the high post of President of the Republic;

121

Taking into consideration that the so-often-repeated Francisco I. Madero has

tried with the brute force of bayonets to shut up and to drown in blood the

pueblos who ask, solicit, or demand from him the fulfillment of the promises of

the revolution, calling them bandits and rebels, condemning them to a war of

extermination without conceding or granting a single one of the guarantees

which reason, justice, and the law prescribe; taking equally into consideration

that the President of the Republic Francisco I. Madero has made of Effective

Suffrage a bloody trick on the people, already against the will of the same

people imposing Attorney José M. Pino Suárez in the Vice-Presidency of the

Republic, or [imposing as] Governors of the States [men] designated by him,

like the so-called General Ambrosio Figueroa, scourge and tyrant of the people

of Morelos, or entering into scandalous cooperation with the científico party,

feudal landlords, and oppressive bosses, enemies of the revolution proclaimed

by him, so as to forge new chains and follow the pattern of a new dictatorship

more shameful and more terrible than that of Porfirio Díaz, for it has been clear

and patent that he has outraged the sovereignty of the States, trampling on the

laws without any respect for lives or interests, as has happened in the State of

Morelos, and others, leading them to the most horrendous anarchy which

contemporary history registers.

For these considerations we declare the aforementioned Francisco I. Madero

inept at realizing the promises of the revolution of which he was the author,

because he has betrayed the principles with which he tricked the will of the

people and was able to get into power: incapable of governing, because he has

no respect for the law and justice of the pueblos, and a traitor to the fatherland,

122

because he is humiliating in blood and fire Mexicans who want liberties, so as to please the científicos, landlords, and bosses who enslave us, and from today on we begin to continue the revolution begun by him, until we achieve the overthrow of the dictatorial powers which exist.

II. Recognition is withdrawn from Sr. Francisco I. Madero as Chief of the Revolution and as President of the Republic, for the reasons which before were expressed, it being attempted to overthrow this official.

III. Recognized as Chief of the Liberating Revolution is the illustrious General Pascual Orozco, the second of the Leader Don Francisco I. Madero, and in case he does not accept this delicate post, recognition as Chief of the Revolution will go to General Don Emiliano Zapata.

IV. The Revolutionary Junta of the State of Morelos manifests to the Nation under formal oath: that it makes its own the plan of San Luis Potosí, with the additions which are expressed below in benefit of the oppressed pueblos, and it will make itself the defender of the principles it defends until victory or death.

V. The Revolutionary Junta of the State of Morelos will admit no transactions or compromises until it achieves the overthrow of the dictatorial elements of Porfirio Díaz and Francisco I. Madero, for the nation is tired of false men and traitors who make promises like liberators and who on arriving in power forget them and constitute themselves as tyrants.

123

VI. As an additional part of the plan we invoke, we give notice: that [regarding] the fields, timber, and water which the landlords, científicos, or bosses have usurped, the pueblos or citizens who have the titles corresponding to those properties will immediately enter into possession of that real estate of which they have been despoiled by the bad faith of our oppressors, maintaining at any cost with arms in hand the mentioned possession; and the usurpers who consider themselves with a right to them [those properties] will deduce it before the special tribunals which will be established on the triumph of the revolution.

VII. In virtue of the fact that the immense majority of Mexican pueblos and citizens are owners of no more than the land they walk on, suffering the horrors of poverty without being able to improve their social condition in any way or to dedicate themselves to Industry or Agriculture, because lands, timber, and water are monopolized in a few hands, for this cause there will be expropriated the third part of those monopolies from the powerful proprietors of them, with prior indemnization, in order that the pueblos and citizens of Mexico may obtain ejidos, colonies, and foundations for pueblos, or fields for sowing or laboring, and the Mexicans' lack of prosperity and well being may improve in all and for all.

VIII. [Regarding] The landlords, científicos, or bosses who oppose the present plan directly or indirectly, their goods will be nationalized and the two third parts which [otherwise would] belong to them will go for indemnizations of war, pensions for widows and orphans of the victims who succumb in the struggle for the present plan.

IX. In order to execute the procedures regarding the properties aforementioned, the laws of disamortization and nationalization will be applied as they fit, for serving us as norm and example can be those laws put in force by the immortal Juárez on ecclesiastical properties, which punished the despots and conservatives who in every time have tried to impose on us the ignominious yoke of oppression and backwardness.

X. The insurgent military chiefs of the Republic who rose up with arms in hand at the voice of Don Francisco I. Madero to defend the plan of San Luis Potosí, and who oppose with armed force the present plan, will be judged traitors to the cause which they defended and to the fatherland, since at present many of them, to humor the tyrants, for a fistful of coins, or for bribes or connivance, are shedding the blood of their brothers who claim the fulfillment of the promises which Don Francisco I. Madero made to the nation.

XI. The expenses of war will be taken in conformity with Article II of the Plan of San Luis Potosí, and all procedures employed in the revolution we undertake will be in conformity with the same instructions which the said plan determines.

XII. Once triumphant the revolution which we carry into the path of reality, a Junta of the principal revolutionary chiefs from the different States will name or designate an interim President of the Republic, who will convoke elections for the organization of the federal powers.

XIII. The principal revolutionary chiefs of each State will designate in Junta the Governor of the State to which they belong, and this appointed official will convoke elections for the due organization of the public powers, the object being to avoid compulsory appointments which work the misfortune of the pueblos, like the so-well-known appointment of Ambrosio Figueroa in the State of Morelos and others who drive us to the precipice of bloody conflicts, sustained by the caprice of the dictator Madero and the circle of científicos and landlords who have influenced him.

XIV. If President Madero and other dictatorial elements of the present and former regime want to avoid the immense misfortunes which afflict the fatherland, and [if they] possess true sentiments of love for it, let them make immediate renunciation of the posts they occupy, and with that, they will with something staunch the grave wounds which they have opened in the bosom of the fatherland, since, if they do not do so, on their heads will fall the blood and the anathema of our brothers.

XV. Mexicans: consider that the cunning and bad faith of one man is shedding blood in a scandalous manner, because he is incapable of governing; consider that his system of government is choking the fatherland and trampling with the brute force of bayonets on our institutions; and thus, as we raised up our weapons to elevate him to power, we again raise them up against him for defaulting on his promises to the Mexican people and for having betrayed the revolution initiated by him, we are not personalists, we are partisans of principles and not of men!

126

Mexican People, support this plan with arms in hand and you will make the prosperity and well being of the fatherland.

Ayala, November 25, 1911.

Liberty, Justice, and Law

Signed, *General in Chief Emiliano Zapata; Generals Eufemio Zapata, Francisco Mendoza, Jesús Morales, Jesús Navarro, Otilio E. Montaño, José Trinidad Ruiz, Próculo Capistrán; Colonels Felipe Vaquero, Cesáreo Burgos, Quintín González, Pedro Salazar, Simón Rojas, Emigdio Marmolejo, José Campos, Pioquinto Galis, Felipe Tijera, Rafael Sánchez, José Pérez, Santiago Aguilar, Margarito Martínez, Feliciano Domínguez, Manuel Vergara, Cruz Salazar, Lauro Sánchez, Amador Salazar, Lorenzo Vázquez, Catarino Perdomo, Jesús Sánchez, Domingo Romero, Zacarías Torres, Bonifacio García, Daniel Andrade, Ponciano Domínguez, Jesús Capistrán; Captains Daniel Mantilla, José M. Carrillo, Francisco Alarcón, Severiano Gutiérrez; and more signatures follow.* [This] is a true copy taken from the original. Camp in the Mountains of Puebla, December 11, 1911. Signed, General in Chief Emiliano Zapata.

Source: John Womack Jr., Zapata and the Mexican Revolution (New York: Vintage Books, 1968), 400-404.

# La Adelita

| | |
|---|---|
| En una alta serranía | On a high mountainside |
| una tropa acampada | a troop,camped |
| una moza los seguía | a girl followed them |
| locamente enamorada | crazily in love |
| Popular entre la tropa era Adelita | Adelita was popular among the troop |
| | |
| la mujer que al sargento le gustaba | the woman that the sargeant liked |
| porque además de ser valiente | because besides being brave |
| era bonita | she was pretty |
| y felizmente para todos trabajaba | and happily worked for everybody |
| | |
| Y se oía que gritaba | And it was heard that somebody was shouting |
| | |
| aquél que tanto le gustaba | that guy that liked her so much |
| y si Adelita fuera mi novia | and if Adelita were my girlfriend |
| y si Adelita fuera mi mujer | and if Adelita were my woman |
| le compraría un vestido de seda | I would buy her a silk dress |
| la llevaría a bailar al cuartel | I would take her dancing at headquarters |
| | |
| Y si Adelita se fuera | And if Adelita were to go |
| con otro | with another guy |
| la seguiría por tierra y por mar | I would follow her by land and by sea |
| | |
| si por mar | if by sea |

| en un buque de Guerra | in a war ship |
| si por tierra | if by land |
| en un tren militar. | in a military train. |

Source: http://www.songsforteaching.com/spanish/laadelita.htm

# CHAPTER 8: WORLD WAR TO COLD WAR

After World War II, Latin American leaders began to consider ways to help their countries develop economically. One of the most important of the new wave of economists was Argentine Raúl Prebisch (1901-1986), who served as the first director of the United Nation's Economic Commission for Latin America (ECLA, often known by its Spanish acronym CEPAL) from 1948-1963. Prebisch's thoughts about the problems that late developing Latin America faced because of its position on the periphery, subjected to the needs of the developed countries at the center, was a trail blazing approach that led the way for the development of Latin American dependency theory, which dominated economic debate through the 1980s.

Many Latin Americans believed, however, felt passionately that the real problem facing Latin America was domination by foreign corporations, with the support of U.S. imperialism. No one expressed this more vividly that Chilean poet Pablo Neruda (1904-1973), whose poem, "The United Fruit Company," was published in 1950.

Neruda seemed prescient when, in 1954, a U.S.-sponsored coup overthrew the reformist government of Jacobo Arbenz in Guatemala. Arbenz instituted an agrarian reform program that targeted the huge stretches of idle land held by Guatemalan coffee growers and by the United Fruit Company. The U.S. justification for supporting action against Guatemala was the supposed threat of international communism, as expressed at a June 28, 1954 meeting of the Organization of American States by the U.S. representative, John C. Dreir.

# Raúl Prebisch: The Periphery v. the Center

In Latin America, reality is undermining the outdated schema of the international division of labor, which achieved great importance in the nineteenth century and, as a theoretical concept, continued to exert considerable influence until very recently.

Under the schema, the specific task that fell to Latin America, as part of the periphery of the world economic system, was that of producing food and raw materials for the great industrial centers.

There was no place within it for the industrialization of the new countries. It is nevertheless being forced upon them by events. Two world wars in a single generation and a great economic crisis between them have shown the Latin American countries their opportunities, clearly pointing the way to industrial activity.

The academic discussion, however, is far from ended. In economics, ideologies usually tend either to lag behind events or to outlive them. It is true that the reasoning on the economic advantages of the international division of labor is theoretically sound, but it is usually forgotten that it is based upon an assumption which has been conclusively proved false by facts. According to this assumption, the benefits of technical progress tend to be distributed alike over the whole community, either by the lowering of prices or by the corresponding raising of incomes. The countries producing raw material obtain their share of these benefits through international exchange, and therefore have no need to industrialize. If they were to do so, their lesser efficiency would result in their losing the conventional advantages of such exchange.

The flaw in this assumption is that of generalizing from the particular. If by "the community" only the great industrial countries are meant, it is indeed true that the benefits of technical progress are gradually distributed among all social groups and classes. If, however, the concept of the community is extended to include the periphery of the world economy, a serious error is implicit in the generalization. The enormous benefits that derive from increased productivity have not reached the periphery in a measure comparable to that obtained by the peoples of the great industrial countries. Hence, the outstanding differences between the standards of living of the masses of the former and the latter and the manifest discrepancies between their respective abilities to accumulate capital, since the margin of savings depends primarily on increased productivity.

Thus there exists and obvious disequilibrium, a fact which, whatever its explanation or justification, destroys the basic premise underlying the schema of the international division
of labor.

Hence, the fundamental significance of the industrialization of the new countries. Industrialization is not an end in itself, but the principal means at the disposal of those countries of obtaining a share of the benefits of technical progress and of progressively raising the standard of living of the masses.

Admittedly much remains to be done in the Latin-American countries, both in learning the facts and in their proper theoretical interpretation. Though many of the problems of these countries are similar, no common effort has ever been made even to examine and elucidate them. It is not surprising, therefore, that the studies published on the economy of Latin American countries often

132

reflect the points of view or the experience of the great centers of world economy. Those studies cannot be expected to solve problems of direct concern to Latin America. The case of the Latin American countries must therefore be presented clearly, so that their interests, aspirations and opportunities, bearing in mind, of course, the individual differences and characteristics, may be adequately integrated within the federal framework of international economic cooperation.

The industrialization of Latin America is not incompatible with the efficient development of primary production. On the contrary, the availability of the best capital equipment and the prompt adoption of new techniques are essential if the development of industry is to fulfill the social objective of raising the standard of living. The same is true of the mechanization of agriculture. Primary products must be exported to allow for the importation of the considerable amount of capital goods needed.

The more active Latin America's foreign trade, the greater the possibility of increasing productivity by means of intensive capital formation. The solution does not lie in growth at the expense of foreign trade, but in knowing how to extract, from continually growing foreign trade, the elements that will promote economic development.

Source: Raúl Prebisch, *The Economic Development of Latin America and its Principal Problems*. Economic Commission for Latin America. 27 April 1950. Lake Success, NY: U.N. Department of Economic Affairs, 1950. Reprinted in *Latin America and the United States: A Documentary History*. Robert H. Holden and Eric Zolov, eds. NY: Oxford University Press, 2000), 199-200.

## John C. Dreier: Communism in the Americas

I speak today as the representative of one of ten American countries who have joined in a request that a Meeting of Ministers of Foreign Affairs be convoked to act as Organ of Consultation under articles 6 and 11 of the Inter-American Treaty of Reciprocal Assistance. On behalf of the United States I wish to support this request with all the force and conviction that I can express, feeling profoundly as I and my countrymen do that this is a critical hour in which a strong and positive note of inter-American solidarity must be sounded.

The Republics of America are faced at this time with a serious threat to their peace and independence. Throughout the world the aggressive forces of Soviet Communist imperialism are exerting a relentless pressure upon all free nations. Since 1939, fifteen once free nations have fallen prey to the forces directed by the Kremlin. Hundreds of millions of people in Europe and Asia have been pressed into the slavery of the Communist totalitarian state. Subversion, civil violence, and open warfare are the proven methods of this aggressive force in its ruthless striving for world domination. The first objectives of this new drive for domination were the countries of Eastern Europe and the Balkins. Communist forces then turned their attention to Asia.

And now comes the attack on America.

There is no doubt that it is the declared policy of the American States that the establishment of a government dominated by the international Communist movement in America would constitute a grave danger to all our American Republics, and that steps must be taken to prevent any such eventuality.

134

I should like to affirm the fact that there is already abundant evidence that the international Communist movement has achieved an extensive preparation of the political institutions of one American State, namely the Republic of Guatemala, and now seeks to exploit that country for its own ends. This assertion, which my Government is prepared to support with convincing detail at the right time, is clearly warranted by the open opposition of the Guatemalan Government to any form of inter-American action that might check or restrain the progress of the international Communist movement in this continent; by the open association of that Government with the policies and objectives of the Soviet Union in international affairs; by the evidences of close collaboration of the authorities in Guatemala and authorities in Soviet-dominated states of Europe for the purpose of obtaining under secret and illegal arrangements the large shipment of arms with arrived on board the HMS *Alfhem* on May 15, 1954; by the efforts of Guatemala in the United Nations Security Council, in collaboration with the Soviet Union, to prevent the Organization of American States, the appropriate regional organization, from dealing with her recent allegations of aggression, and finally by the vigorous and sustained propaganda campaign of the Soviet press and radio, echoed by the international Communist propaganda machine throughout the world in support of Guatemalan action in the present crisis.

I should like to emphasize the fact that the object of our concern, and the force against which we must take defensive measures, is an alien, non-American force. It is the international Communist organization controlled in the Kremlin which has created the present danger. We are confident that the international Communist movement holds no real appeal for the peoples of

America and can only subdue them if allowed to pursue its violent and deceitful methods unchecked. Having read the tragic history of other nations seduced by Communist promises into a slavery from which they later could not escape, we wish to leave no stone unturned, no effort unexerted, to prevent the complete subordination of one of our member states to Soviet Communist imperialism.

Source:  U.S. Department of State. "The Guatemalan Problem Before the OAS Council.  In *Intervention of International Communism in Guatemala.* Department of State Publication 5556, Inter-American Series 48. Released August 1954, 25-30.  Washington, D.C.: GPO, 1954.  Reprinted in *Latin America and the United States: A Documentary History.*  Robert H. Holden and Eric Zolov, eds.  N.Y.: Oxford University Press, 2000, 201-203.

## Pablo Neruda, The United Fruit Company

When the trumpet sounded, everything

on earth was prepared

and Jehovah distributed the world

to Coca Cola Inc., Anaconda,

Ford Motors and other entities:

The Fruit Company Inc.

reserved the juiciest for itself,

the central coast of my land,

the sweet waist of America.

It re-baptized the lands

"Banana Republics"

and on the sleeping dead,

on the restless heroes

who'd conquered greatness,

liberty and flags,

it founded a comic opera:

it alienated free wills,

gave crowns of Caesar as gifts,

unsheathed jealousy, attracted

the dictatorship of the flies,

Trujillo flies, Tacho flies,

Carias flies, Martinez flies,

Ubico flies, flies soppy

with humble blood and marmelade,

drunken flies that buzz

around common graves,

circus flies, learned flies

adept at tyranny.


The Company disembarks

among the blood-thirsty flies,

brim-filling their boats that slide

with the coffee and fruit treasure

of our submerged lands like trays.


Meanwhile, along the sugared up

abysms of the ports,

indians fall over, buried

in the morning mist:

a body rolls, a thing

without a name, a fallen number,

a bunch of dead fruit

spills into the pile of rot.


Source: Translated by Jack Hirschman from *The Essential Neruda,*

http://www.redpoppy.net/

# CHAPTER 9: THE REVOLUTIONARY OPTION

Fidel Castro became a hero to much of Latin America when he led Cuba in a successful revolution in 1959, toppling dictator Fulgencio Batista. Castro's first attempt to overthrow the dictatorship came in the attack on the Moncada garrison on July 26, 1953. Castro, an attorney, represented himself at trial, in a characteristically long, extemporaneous presentation. Legend has it that he later transcribed his testimony from memory, writing in lemon juice on scraps of paper smuggled out of prison, then typed and printed by supporters in Havana. The speech has become known by its closing line: "History will absolve me."

The Cuban revolution inspired Nicolás Guillén (1902-1989), who was one of Latin America's most important poets long before 1959. Guillén first made his mark in the world of poetry in 1930. He embraced the revolution, becoming its poet laureate, and particularly wrote about the revolution's commitment to improving the conditions of Afro-Cubans.

Nicaraguans pride themselves on being a nation of poets. It was a poet who killed the first Somoza, and poets were active in the Sandinista revolution. Leonél Rugama (1950-1970) was a native of Estelí, Nicaragua, who joined the *Frente Sandinista de LiberaciónNational* (FSLN) in 1967 and was killed in a shootout with the National Guard in 1970. Rugama insisted that the role of everyone in a repressive society—but particularly of the student, the intellectual, and the poet—was to make revolution, in word and in deed.

# Fidel Castro: History Will Absolve Me

The article in question reads textually: "A penalty of imprisonment of from three to ten years shall be imposed upon the perpetrator of any act aimed at bringing about an armed uprising against the Constitutional Powers of the State. The penalty shall be imprisonment for from five to twenty years, in the event that insurrection actually be carried into effect."

In what country is the Honorable Prosecutor living? Who has told him that we have sought to bring about an uprising against the Constitutional Powers of the State? Two things are self-evident. First of all, the dictatorship that oppresses the nation is not a constitutional power, but an unconstitutional one: it was established against the Constitution, over the head of the Constitution, violating the legitimate Constitution of the Republic. The legitimate Constitution is that which emanates directly from a sovereign people. Secondly, the article refers to Powers, in the plural, as in the case of a republic governed by a Legislative Power, an Executive Power, and a Judicial Power which balance and counterbalance one another. We have fomented a rebellion against one single power, an illegal one, which has usurped and merged into a single whole both the Legislative and Executive Powers of the nation, and so has destroyed the entire system that was specifically safeguarded by the Code now under our analysis. No matter how Article 148 may be stretched, shrunk, or amended, not a single comma applies to the events of July 26th.

The five revolutionary laws that would have been proclaimed immediately after the capture of the Moncada Barracks and would have been broadcast to the nation by radio must be included in the indictment.

140

The first revolutionary law would have returned power to the people and proclaimed the 1940 Constitution the Supreme Law of the State until such time as the people should decide to modify or change it.

The second revolutionary law would give non-mortgageable and non-transferable ownership of the land to all tenant and subtenant farmers, lessees, share croppers and squatters who hold parcels of five *caballerías* of land or less, and the State would indemnify the former owners on the basis of the rental which they would have received for these parcels over a period of ten years.

The third revolutionary law would have granted workers and employees the right to share thirty percent of the profits of all the large industrial, mercantile and mining enterprises, including the sugar mills. The strictly agricultural enterprises would be exempt in consideration of other agrarian laws which would be put into effect.

The fourth revolutionary law would have granted all sugar planters the right to share fifty five percent of sugar production and a minimum quota of forty thousand arrobas for all small tenant farmers who have been established for three years or more.

The fifth revolutionary law would have ordered the confiscation of all holdings and ill-gotten gains of those who had committed frauds during previous regimes, as well as the holdings and ill-gotten gains of all their legates and heirs. To implement this, special courts with full powers would gain access to all records of all corporations registered or operating in this country, in order to investigate concealed funds of illegal origin, and to request that foreign governments extradite persons and attach holdings rightfully belonging to the Cuban people. Half of the property recovered would be used to subsidize

141

retirement funds for workers and the other half would be used for hospitals, asylums and charitable organizations.

Furthermore, it was declared that the Cuban policy in the Americas would be one of close solidarity with the democratic peoples of this continent, and that all those politically persecuted by bloody tyrannies oppressing our sister nations would find generous asylum, brotherhood and bread in the land of Martí; not the persecution, hunger and treason they find today. Cuba should be the bulwark of liberty and not a shameful link in the chain of despotism.

All these laws and others would be based on the exact compliance of two essential articles of our Constitution: one of them orders the outlawing of large estates, indicating the maximum area of land any one person or entity may own for each type of agricultural enterprise by adopting measures which would tend to revert the land to the Cubans. The other categorically orders the State to use all means at its disposal to provide employment to all those who lack it and to ensure a decent livelihood to each manual or intellectual laborer. None of these laws can be called unconstitutional. The first popularly elected government would have to respect them, not only because of moral obligations to the nation, but because when people achieve something they have yearned for throughout generations, no force in the world is capable of taking it away again.

The problem of the land, the problem of industrialization, the problem of housing, the problem of unemployment, the problem of education and the problem of the people's health: these are the six problems we would take immediate steps to solve, along with restoration of civil liberties and political democracy.

This exposition may seem cold and theoretical if one does not know the shocking and tragic conditions of the country with regard to these six problems, along with the most humiliating political oppression.

Eighty-five per cent of the small farmers in Cuba pay rent and live under constant threat of being evicted from the land they till. More than half of our most productive land is in the hands of foreigners. In Oriente, the largest province, the lands of the United Fruit Company and the West Indian Company link the northern and southern coasts. There are two hundred thousand peasant families who do not have a single acre of land to till to provide food for their starving children. On the other hand, nearly three hundred thousand *caballerías* of cultivatable land owned by powerful interests remain uncultivated. If Cuba is above all an agricultural State, if its population is largely rural, if the city depends on these rural areas, if the people from our countryside won our war of independence, if our nation's greatness and prosperity depend on a healthy and vigorous rural population that loves the land and knows how to work it, if this population depends on a State that protects and guides it, then how can the present state of affairs be allowed to continue?

To those who would call me a dreamer, I quote the words of Martí: "A true man does not seek the path where advantage lies, but rather the path where duty lies," and this is the only practical man, whose dream of today will be the law of tomorrow, because he who has looked back on the essential course of history and has seen flaming and bleeding peoples seethe in the cauldron of the ages knows that, without a single exception, the future lies on the side of duty. I do not fear prison, as I do not fear the fury of the miserable tyrant who took the lives of seventy of my comrades. Condemn me. It does not matter. History will

absolve me.

Source: Fidel Castro, *History Will Absolve Me*,

http://www.marxists.org/history/cuba/archive/castro/1953/10/16.htm

### Nicolás Guillén: I Have

When I look at and touch myself,

I, John-only-yesterday-with-Nothing

and John-with-everything-today,

with everything today,

I glance around, I look and see

and touch myself and wonder

how it could have happened.

I have, let's see:

I have the pleasure of walking my country,

the owner of all there is in it,

examining at very close range what

I could not and did not have before.

I can say cane,

I can say mountain,

I can say city,

I can say army,

army say,

now mine forever and yours, ours,

and the vast splendor of

the sunbeam, the star, the flower.

I have, let's see:

I have the pleasure of going,

me, a peasant, a worker, a simple man,

I have the pleasure of going

(just an example)

to a bank and speaking to the manager,

not in English,

not in "Sir,"

but in *compañero* as we say in Spanish.

I have, let's see:

that being Black

I can be stopped by no one at

the door of a dancing hall or bar.

Or even at the desk of a hotel

have someone yell at me there are no rooms,

a small room and not one that's immense,

a tiny room where I might rest.

I have, let's see:

that there are no rural police

to seize me and lock me in a precinct jail,

or tear me from my land and cast me

in the middle of the highway.

I have that having the land I have the sea,

no country clubs,

no high life,

no tennis and no yachts,

but, from beach to beach and wave on wave,

gigantic blue open democratic:

in short, the sea.

I have, let's see:

that I have learned to read,

to count,

I have that I have learned to write,

and to think

and to laugh.

I have that now I have

a place to work

and earn

what I have to eat.

I have, let's see:

I have what was coming to me.

## Leonél Rugama: The Earth Is a Satellite of the Moon

Apollo 2 cost more than Apollo 1

Apollo 1 cost plenty.

Apollo 3 cost more than Apollo 2

Apollo 2 cost more than Apollo 1

Apollo 1 cost plenty.

Apollo 4 cost more than Apollo 3

Apollo 3 cost more than Apollo 2

Apollo 2 cost more than Apollo 1

Apollo 1 cost plenty.

Apollo 8 cost a fortune, but no one minded

because the astronauts were Protestant

they read the Bible from the moon

astounding and delighting every Christian

and on their return Pope Paul VI gave them his blessing.

Apollo 9 cost more than all these put together

including Apollo 1 which cost plenty.

The great-grandparents of the people of Acahualinca were less

hungry than the grandparents.

The great-grandparents died of hunger.

The grandparents of the people of Acahualinca were less

hungry than the parents.

The grandparents died of hunger.

The parents of the people of Acahualinca were less

hungry than the children of the people there.

The parents died of hunger.

The people of Acahualinca are less hungry than the children

of the people there.

The children of the people of Acahualinca, because of hunger,

are not born

they hunger to be born, only to die of hunger.

Blessed are the poor for they shall inherit the moon.

Source: Leonel Rugama, *The Earth Is a Satellite of the Moon*. Sara Miles, Richard Schaaf, and Nancy Weisberg, tran. (Willimantic, CT: Curbstone Press, 1984), 11, 13.

# CHAPTER 10: DEBT AND DICTATORSHIP

The revolutionary movements of the 1970s were profoundly influenced by liberation theology. The doctrine had its roots in the 1960s, when Vatican's Council II (1962-65) expressed concern for a more democratic Church and for greater social and economic justice. This commitment was expressed at Second General Conference of Latin American Bishops meeting in Medellín, Colombia, in 1968, and expressed in the Medellín Document on Peace.

Priests, however, were among those targeted by the military dictatorships that dominated Latin America in the 1970s and the early 1980s. By the middle of the decade, as civilian governments were elected, they formed commissions to investigate the reports of kidnapping and torture. The results shocked people within these countries and around the world. The reports revealed that the armed forces of these Latin American countries were trained to torture people, and they carried out this torture systematically in such countries as Argentina, Brazil, and Guatemala.

# Medellín Document on Peace: Pastoral Conclusions

XX. In the face of the tensions which conspire against peace, and even present the temptation of violence; in the face of the Christian concept of peace which has been described, we believe that the Latin American Episcopate cannot avoid assuming very concrete responsibilities, because to create a just social order, without which peace is illusory, is an eminently Christian task.

To us, the pastors of the church, belongs the duty to educate the Christian conscience, to inspire, stimulate, and help orient all of the initiatives that contribute to the formation of man. It is also up to us to denounce everything which, opposing justice, destroys peace.

In this spirit we feel it opportune to bring up the following pastoral points:

XXI. To awaken in individuals and communities, principally through mass media, a living awareness of justice, infusing in them a dynamic sense of responsibility and solidarity.

XXII. To defend the rights of the poor and oppressed according to the gospel commandment, urging our governments and upper classes to eliminate anything which might destroy social peace: injustice, inertia, venality, insensibility.

XXIII. To favor integration, energetically denouncing the abuses and unjust consequences of the excessive inequalities between rich and poor, weak and powerful.

XXIV. To be certain that our preaching, liturgy, and catechesis take into account the social and community dimensions of Christianity, forming men committed to world peace.

XXV. To achieve in our schools, seminaries, and universities a healthy critical sense of the social situation and foster the vocation of service. We also consider very efficacious the diocesan and national campaigns that mobilize the faithful and social organizations, leading them to a similar reflection.

XXVI. To invite various Christian and non-Christian communities to collaborate in this fundamental task of our times.

XXVII. To encourage and favor the efforts of the people to create and develop their own grass-roots organizations for the redress and consolidation of their rights and the search for true justice.

XXVIII. To request the perfecting of the administration of justice, whose deficiencies often cause serious ills.

XXIX. To urge a halt and revision in many of our countries of the arms race that at times constitutes a burden excessively disproportionate to the legitimate demands of the common good, to the detriment of desperate social necessities. The struggle against misery is the true war that our nations should face.

XXX. To invite the bishops, the leaders of different churches, and all men of good will of the developed nations to promote in their respective spheres of influence, especially among the political and financial leaders, a consciousness of greater solidarity facing our underdeveloped nations, obtaining, among other things, just prices for our raw materials.

XXXI. On the occasion of the twentieth anniversary of the solemn declaration of Human Rights, to interest universities in Latin America to undertake investigations to verify the degree of its implementation in our countries.

XXXII. To denounce the unjust action of world powers that works against self-determination of weaker nations who must suffer the bloody consequences of war and invasion, and to ask competent international organizations for effective and decisive procedures.

XXXIII. To encourage and praise the initiatives and works of all those who in the diverse areas of action contribute to the creation of a new order which will assure peace in our midst.

Source: The Church in the Present-Day Transformation of Latin America in the Light of the Council, II, Conclusions (Bogotá: General Secretariat of CELAM, 1970), 71-82. Reprinted in *Third World Liberation Theologies, A Reader.* Deane William Ferm, ed. Maryknoll, NY: Orbis Books, 1986), 9-10.

# Never Again: Reports on Torturers in Argentina, Brazil and Guatemala

## *Argentina*

Many of the events described in this report will be hard to believe. This is because the men and women of our nation have only heard of such horror in reports from distant places. The enormity of what took place in Argentina, involving the transgression of the most fundamental human rights, is sure, still, to produce that disbelief which some used at the time to defend themselves from pain and horror. In so doing, they also avoided the responsibility born of knowledge and awareness, because the question necessarily follows: how can we prevent it happening again? And the frightening realization that both the victims and their tormentors were our contemporaries, that the tragedy took place on our soil, and that those who insulted the history of our country in this way have yet to show by word or deed that they feel any remorse for what they have done.

*Carlos Alberto Campero (file No. 1806) relates the following unforgettable episode:*

> My mother was taken to the shop and, threatening her life, they beat her in a way that should not even be used on wild animals. In the shop we had a ventilator fan. They cut the cable, plugged it in and used it to give her electric shocks. So that it would have more effect, they poured mineral water over my mother, whom they had tied to a chair. While they were committing this savagery, another one of them was beating her with a belt until her body was bleeding and her face disfigured. After some considerable time they decided to take

us all with them, except for the six month old Viviana, who was left behind with Griselda, my thirteen year old sister.

*Dr. Norberto Liwsky (file No. 7397)...*

For days they applied electric shocks to my gums, nipples, genitals, abdomen and ears. They then began to beat me systematically and rhythmically with wooden sticks on my back, the backs of my thighs, my calves and the soles of my feet. At first the pain was dreadful. Then it became unbearable. Eventually I lost all feeling in the part of my body being beaten. The agonizing pain returned a short while after they finished hitting me. It was made still worse when they tore off my shirt, which had stuck to the wounds. In between torture sessions they left me hanging by my arms from hooks fixed in the wall of the cell where they had thrown me.

## Brazil

Dulce Chaves Pandolfi, student, 24, was obliged to serve as a guinea pig in the barracks on Barão de Mesquita Street, in Rio, according to a statement attached to military court records dates 1970:

At the Military Police, the defendant was stripped naked and subjected to beatings and electric shocks and other torments such as the "parrot's perch." After being taken to her cell, the defendant was assisted by a doctor and, after a while, was again tortured with exquisite cruelty in a demonstration of how torture should be carried out.

The torturers not only bragged about their sophisticated technology of pain, but boasted that they were in a position to export it to repressive systems in other countries.

This was stated in a letter from Haroldo Borges Rodrigues Lima, engineer, 37, dated 12 April 1977 and appended to military court records:

Tortures continued systematically. They were accompanied by threats to subject me to new and harsher torments, which were described to me in detail. They said, with great pride, that in this matter they owed nothing to any foreign organization. On the contrary, they told me, they were already exporting know-how on the subject.

*The "parrot's perch".*

The parrot's perch consists of an iron bar wedged behind the victim's knees and to which his wrists are tied; the bar is then placed between two tables, causing the victim's body to hang some 20 to 30 centimeters from the ground. This method is hardly ever used by itself: its normal "complements" are electric shocks, the pamatória [a length of thick rubber attached to a wooden paddle], and drowning.

[Augusto César Salles Galvão, student, 21, Belo Horizonte, 1970]

*Insects and Animals*

There was also, in his cubicle, to keep him company, a boa constrictor called "Miriam".

[Leonardo Valentini]

The defendant also wants to state that, during the first phase of her interrogation, cockroaches were placed over her body, and one of them into her anus.

[Lúcia Maria Murat Vasconcelos, 23, student, Rio and Salvador, 1972.]

When José Leão Carvalho, advertising agent, was detained in São Paulo, on 24 June 1964, his children were not spared:

making threats to this younger children, which resulted in the boy

Sérgio having to have medical-psychiatric treatment. He was three

years old at that time.

In 1973, in Rio, the military court heard the testimony of Maria da Conceição

Chaves Fernandes, proofreader, 19:

that she was subjected to sexual violence in the presence and in the

absence of her husband.

## Guatemala

The strategy of terror in Guatemala degenerated into the most extreme

displays of disregard for human life with public torture sessions, public display

of corpses, and the appearance of mutilated bodies bearing signs of torture.

*They had cut out his tongue. His eyes were blindfolded with a*

*wide bandage or wide tape and there were punctures*

*everywhere on his rib cage, and it seemed that one of his arms*

*was broken. They left him unrecognizable. And I could tell it*

*was him only because I had lived with him for many years and*

*I knew about certain scars.* Case 30310. Cuilapa, Santa Rosa,

1981.

*The soldiers had begun to kill, without a word. They weren't*

*asking whether anyone had done anything wrong or not; they*

*were killing that day.* Case 6629, Alta Verapaz, 1981.

*It was necessary to leave the ancestors behind, the dead were*

*far away, the sacred sites too.* Case 569, Cobán, Alta

Verapaz, 1981.

*Well, the told my sister–since among the soldiers there was*

*one who spoke our language–and he told my sister that they*

*had to finish off all the men and all the male children in order*

*to eliminate the guerrillas. "And why?" she asked, "and why*

*are you killing the children?" "Because those wretches are*

*going to come some day and screw us over." That was their*

*intention when they killed the little ones too.* Case 1944,

Chiché, Quiché, 1983.

Source: *Nunca Más: The Report of the Argentine National Commission on the Disappeared.* (NY: Farrar Straus Giroux, 1986), 9, 18, 20, 22. *Torture in Brazil: A Shocking Report on the Pervasive Use of Torture by Brazilian Military Governments, 1964-1979.* (Secretly prepared by the Archdiocese of São Paulo. Jaime Wright, tran. Austin: University of Texas Press, 1985), 14-15, 16, 21-22, 27, 30. *Guatemala: Never Again! The Official Report of the Human Rights Office, Archdiocese of Guatemala.* (Maryknoll, NY: Orbis Books, 1999), 7, 9, 14, 31.

# CHAPTER 11: FORWARD INTO THE PAST

One of the best ways to gauge conditions in Latin America in the $21^{st}$ century is to look at the statistics on economic and social development. The raw data for the tables in this section comes from the CIA Word Fact Book, which in turn draws its data from the agencies in each country that generate the data. The tables compiled here are not identical–there are categories in 2005 that were not reported in 2000. The data are testimony to continuing problems with poverty and world trade.

It is concern with such problems that have catapulted a new generation of leaders to prominence. Hugo Chávez (1954-) tried to take over the government of Venezuela in a coup in 1992. He succeeded in taking the helm via elections in 1998. He has become one of the most important in a new crop of Latin American leaders who advocate revolutionary changes through elected governments. Chavez's popularity was evident as he spoke in 2005 at the World Social Forum, which has become a significant world summit for voices the concerns of what used to be called the Third World.

José Emilio Pacheco (1939) has been described as "the most important Mexican poet of the generation following Octavio Paz." His work has been hailed as the first of Latin America's post-modern writing. Pacheco demands an active reader who participates in the process as he tries to find meaning in the fractured, de-centered world of the late twentieth and early twenty-first centuries.

# STATISTICS ON LATIN AMERICA AND THE UNITED STATES, 2005

| Country | Population (Millions) | Population Growth Rate | Infant Mortality per 1,000 Live Births | Fertility Rate | Life Expectancy | Literacy | GDP per Capita Purchasing Power Parity | Population Below Poverty Level |
|---|---|---|---|---|---|---|---|---|
| Argentina | 39,537,943 | 0.98% | 15.18 | 2.19 | 75.9 | 97.1% | $12,400 | 44.3% |
| Bolivia | 8,857,870 | 1.49 | 53.11 | 2.94 | 65.5 | 87.2 | 2,600 | 64.0 |
| Brazil | 186,112,794 | 1.06 | 29.61 | 1.93 | 71.69 | 86.4 | 8,100 | 22.0 |
| Chile | 15,980,912 | 0.97 | 8.8 | 2.02 | 76.58 | 96.2 | 10,700 | 20.6 |
| Colombia | 42,954,279 | 1.49 | 20.97 | 2.56 | 71.72 | 92.5 | 6,600 | 55.0 |
| Costa Rica | 4,016,173 | 1.48 | 9.95 | 2.28 | 76.84 | 95.9 | 9,600 | 18.0 |
| Cuba | 11,346,670 | 0.33 | 6.33 | 1.66 | 77.23 | 97.0 | 3,000 | NA |
| Dominican Republic | 8,950,034 | 1.29 | 32.38 | 2.86 | 67.26 | 84.7 | 6,300 | 25.0 |
| Ecuador | 13,363,593 | 1.24 | 23.66 | 2.72 | 76.21 | 92.5 | 3,700 | 45.0 |
| El Salvador | 6,704,932 | 1.75 | 25.1 | 3.16 | 71.22 | 80.2 | 4,900 | 36.1 |
| Guatemala | 14,655,189 | 2.57 | 35.93 | 4.53 | 65.14 | 70.6 | 4,200 | 75.0 |
| Honduras | 6,975,204 | 2.16 | 29.32 | 3.87 | 65.6 | 76.2 | 2,800 | 53.0 |
| Mexico | 106,202,903 | 1.17 | 20.91 | 2.45 | 75.19 | 92.2 | 9,600 | 40.0 |
| Nicaragua | 5,465,100 | 1.92 | 29.11 | 2.81 | 70.33 | 67.5 | 2,300 | 50.0 |
| Panama | 3,039,150 | 1.26 | 20.47 | 2.45 | 71.94 | 92.6 | 6,900 | 37.0 |
| Paraguay | 6,347,884 | 2.48 | 25.63 | 3.93 | 74.89 | 94.0 | 4,800 | 36.0 |
| Peru | 27,925,628 | 1.36 | 31.94 | 2.56 | 69.53 | 90.9 | 5,600 | 54.0 |
| Uruguay | 3,415,920 | 0.47 | 11.95 | 1.91 | 76.13 | 98.0 | 14,500 | 21.0 |
| Venezuela | 25,375,281 | 1.4 | 22.2 | 2.26 | 74.31 | 93.4 | 5,800 | 47.0 |
| United States | 295,734,134 | 0.92 | 6.5 | 2.08 | 77.71 | 97.0 | 40,100 | 12.0 |

| Country | GDP by sector | | | GDP Real Growth | Unemployment Rate | Exports (in billions) | Imports (in billions) | External Debt (in billions) |
|---|---|---|---|---|---|---|---|---|
| | Agriculture | Industry | Service | | | | | |
| Argentina | 7.0 | 29.0 | 64.0 | -3.0 | 14.0 | $23.0 | $25.0 | $149.0 |
| Bolivia | 16.6 | 35.5 | 47.9 | 2.0 | 11.4 | 1.1 | 1.6 | 5.7 |
| Brazil | 14.0 | 36.0 | 50.0 | 0.8 | 7.5 | 46.9 | 48.7 | 200.0 |
| Chile | 6.0 | 33.0 | 61.0 | 1.1 | 9.0 | 15.6 | 13.9 | 39.0 |
| Colombia | 19.0 | 26.0 | 55.0 | -5.0 | 20.0 | 11.5 | 10.0 | 35.0 |
| Costa Rica | 14.0 | 22.0 | 64.0 | 7.9 | 5.6 | 6.4 | 6.5 | 3.9 |
| Cuba | 7.4 | 36.5 | 56.1 | 6.2 | 6.0 | 1.4 | 3.2 | 11.2 |
| Dominican Republic | 13.6 | 30.8 | 55.6 | 8.3 | 13.8 | 5.1 | 8.2 | 3.7 |
| Ecuador | 14.0 | 36.0 | 50.0 | -8.0 | 12.0 | 4.1 | 2.8 | 15.3 |
| El Salvador | 12.0 | 22.0 | 66.0 | 2.2 | 7.7 | 2.5 | 4.15 | 3.3 |
| Guatemala | 23.0 | 20.0 | 57.0 | 3.5 | 7.5 | 2.4 | 4.5 | 4.4 |
| Honduras | 20.0 | 25.0 | 55.0 | -3.0 | 12.0 | 1.6 | 2.7 | 4.4 |
| Mexico | 5.0 | 29.0 | 66.0 | 3.7 | 2.5 | 136.8 | 142.1 | 155.8 |
| Nicaragua | 34.0 | 22.0 | 44.0 | 6.3 | 10.5 | 0.57 | 1.5 | 5.7 |
| Panama | 8.0 | 25.0 | 67.0 | 4.4 | 13.1 | 4.7 | 6.4 | 7.0 |
| Paraguay | 28.0 | 21.0 | 51.0 | -1.0 | 12.0 | 3.1 | 3.2 | 2.7 |
| Peru | 13.0 | 42.0 | 45.0 | 2.4 | 7.7 | 5.9 | 8.4 | 31.0 |
| Uruguay | 10.0 | 28.0 | 62.0 | -2.5 | 12.0 | 2.1 | 3.4 | 8.0 |
| Venezuela | 4.0 | 63.0 | 33.0 | -7.2 | 18.0 | 20.9 | 11.8 | 32.0 |
| United States | 2.0 | 18.0 | 80.0 | 4.1 | 4.2 | 663.0 | 912.0 | 862.0 |

| Country | Household Income | | Telephones | | Internet Hosts | Internet Users |
|---|---|---|---|---|---|---|
| | Top 10% | Bottom 10% | Main lines | Cellular | | |
| Argentina | NA | NA | 8,009,400 | 6,500,000 | 742,358 | 4,100,000 |
| Bolivia | 32.0 | 1.3 | 600,100 | 1,401,500 | 7,080 | 270,000 |
| Brazil | 48.0 | 0.7 | 38,810,000 | 46,373,300 | 3,163,349 | 14,300,000 |
| Chile | 47.0 | 1.2 | 3,467,000 | 6,445,700 | 202,429 | 3,575,000 |
| Colombia | 44.0 | 1.0 | 8,768,100 | 6,186,200 | 115,158 | 2,732,200 |
| Costa Rica | 36.8 | 1.1 | 1,132,000 | 528,047 | 10,826 | 800,000 |
| Cuba | NA | NA | 574,400 | 17,900 | 1,529 | 120,000 |
| Dominican Republic | 37.9 | 2.1 | 901,800 | 2,120,400 | 64,197 | 500,000 |
| Ecuador | 32.0 | 2.0 | 1,549,000 | 2,394,400 | 3,188 | 569,700 |
| El Salvador | 39.3 | 1.4 | 752,600 | 1,149,800 | 4,084 | 550,000 |
| Guatemala | 46.0 | 1.6 | 846,000 | 1,577,100 | 20,360 | 400,000 |
| Honduras | 42.7 | 0.6 | 322,500 | 326,500 | 1,944 | 168,600 |
| Mexico | 35.6 | 106 | 15,958,700 | 28,125,000 | 1,333,406 | 10,033,000 |
| Nicaragua | 45.0 | 1.2 | 171,600 | 202,800 | 7,094 | 90,000 |
| Panama | 35.7 | 1.2 | 386,900 | 834,000 | 7,129 | 120,000 |
| Paraguay | 43.8 | 0.5 | 273,200 | 1,770,300 | 9,243 | 120,000 |
| Peru | 37.2 | 0.8 | 1,839,200 | 2,908,800 | 65,868 | 2,085,000 |
| Uruguay | 25.8 | 3.7 | 946,500 | 652,000 | 87,630 | 400,000 |
| Venezuela | 36.5 | 0.8 | 2,841,800 | 6,463,600 | 35,301 | 1,274,400 |
| United States | 30.5 | 1.8 | 181,599,900 | 158,722,000 | 115,311,958 | 159,000,000 |

Source:  Date from *The World Factbook* 2005, Washington, D.C.: Central Intelligence Agency, 2005. http://www.cia.gov/cia/publications/factbook/index.html

## STATISTICS ON THE NATIONS OF LATIN AMERICA AND THE UNITED STATES, 2000

| Country | Population (Millions) | Population Growth Rate | Infant Mortality per 1,000 Live Births | Fertility Rate | Life Expectancy | Literacy | GDP per Capita Purchasing Power Parity | Population Below Poverty Level |
|---|---|---|---|---|---|---|---|---|
| Argentina | 36,955,182 | 1.16% | 18.31 | 2.47 | 75.05 | 96.2 | $10,000 | 36.0% |
| Bolivia | 8,152,620 | 1.83 | 60.44 | 3.66 | 63.7 | 83.1 | 3,000 | 70.0 |
| Brazil | 172,860,370 | 0.94 | 38.04 | 2.13 | 62.94 | 83.3 | 6,150 | 17.4 |
| Chile | 15,153,797 | 0.97 | 9.6 | 2.2 | 75.74 | 95.2 | 12,400 | 22.0 |
| Colombia | 39,685,655 | 1.68 | 24.7 | 2.69 | 70.28 | 91.3 | 6,200 | 17.7 |
| Costa Rica | 3,710,558 | 1.69 | 11.49 | 2.52 | 75.82 | 94.8 | 7,100 | NA |
| Cuba | 11,141,997 | 0.39 | 7.5 | 1.60 | 76.21 | 95.7 | 1,700 | NA |
| Dominican Republic | 8,442,533 | 1.64 | 35.93 | 3.0 | 73.2 | 82.1 | 5,400 | 25.0 |
| Ecuador | 12,920,092 | 2.04 | 35.13 | 3.18 | 71.06 | 90.1 | 4,300 | 50.0 |
| El Salvador | 6,122,515 | 1.87 | 29.22 | 3.38 | 69.74 | 71.5 | 3,100 | 48.0 |
| Guatemala | 12,639,939 | 2.63 | 47.0 | 4.66 | 66.18 | 55.6 | 3,900 | 75.0 |
| Honduras | 6,249,598 | 2.52 | 31.29 | 4.26 | 69.93 | 72.7 | 2,050 | 50.0 |
| Mexico | 100,349,766 | 1.53 | 26.19 | 2.67 | 71.49 | 89.6 | 8,500 | 27.0 |
| Nicaragua | 4,812,569 | 2.2 | 34.79 | 3.27 | 68.74 | 65.7 | 2,650 | 50.0 |
| Panama | 2,808,268 | 1.34 | 20.80 | 2.32 | 75.47 | 90.8 | 7,600 | NA |
| Paraguay | 5,585,828 | 2.64 | 30.80 | 4.16 | 73.68 | 92.1 | 3,650 | 32.0 |
| Peru | 27,012,899 | 1.75 | 40.60 | 3.04 | 70.01 | 88.8 | 4,400 | 54.0 |
| Uruguay | 3,334,074 | 0.77 | 15.14 | 2.37 | 75.24 | 97.3 | 8,500 | NA |
| Venezuela | 23,542,649 | 1.60 | 26.17 | 2.51 | 73.07 | 91.1 | 8,000 | 67.0 |
| United States | 275,562,673 | 0.91 | 6.82 | 2.06 | 77.12 | 97.0 | 33,900 | 12.7 |

| Country | GDP by Sector | | | GDP Real Growth | Unemployment Rate [underemployment] | Exports (in billions) | Imports (in billions) | External Debt (in billions) |
|---|---|---|---|---|---|---|---|---|
| | Agriculture | Industry | Service | | | | | |
| Argentina | 10.6 | 35.9 | 53.5 | 8.3 | 14.8 | $33.78 | $22.1 | $157.7 |
| Bolivia | 13.0 | 28.0 | 59.0 | 3.7 | 9.2 [widespread] | 1.9 | 1.6 | 5.4 |
| Brazil | 10.1 | 38.6 | 51.3 | 5.1 | 11.5 | 95.0 | 61.0 | 219.8 |
| Chile | 6.3 | 38.2 | 55.5 | 5.8 | 8.5 | 29.2 | 22.53 | 44.6 |
| Colombia | 13.4 | 32.1 | 54.5 | 3.6 | 13.6 | 15.5 | 15.34 | 38.7 |
| Costa Rica | 8.5 | 29.7 | 61.8 | 3.9 | 6.6 | 6.184 | 7.842 | 5.962 |
| Cuba | 6.6 | 25.5 | 67.9 | 3.0 | 2.5 | 2.104 | 5.296 | 12.09 |
| Dominican Republic | 10.7 | 31.5 | 57.8 | 1.7 | 17.0 | 5.446 | 8.093 | 7.745 |
| Ecuador | 8.7 | 30.5 | 60.9 | 5.8 | 11.1 [47.0] | 7.56 | 7.65 | 16.81 |
| El Salvador | 9.2 | 31.1 | 59.7 | 1.8 | 6.3 [much] | 3.249 | 5.968 | 4.792 |
| Guatemala | 22.7 | 19.5 | 57.9 | 2.6 | 7.5 | 2.911 | 7.77 | 5.969 |
| Honduras | 12.7 | 32.1 | 55.3 | 4.2 | 28.5 | 1.457 | 3.332 | 5.365 |
| Mexico | 4.0 | 27.2 | 68.9 | 4.1 | 3.2 [25.0] | 182.4 | 190.8 | 149.9 |
| Nicaragua | 20.7 | 24.7 | 54.6 | 4.0 | 7.8 [46.5] | 0.750 | 2.02 | 4.573 |
| Panama | 7.2 | 13.0 | 79.8 | 6.0 | 12.6 | 5.699 | 7.164 | 8.78 |
| Paraguay | 25.3 | 24.9 | 49.8 | 2.8 | 15.1 | 2.936 | 3.33 | 3.239 |
| Peru | 8.0 | 27.0 | 65.0 | 4.5 | 9.6 [widespread] | 12.3 | 9.6 | 29.79 |
| Uruguay | 7.9 | 27.4 | 64.8 | 10.2 | 13.0 | 2.2 | 2.071 | 12.8 |
| Venezuela | 0.1 | 46.5 | 53.4 | 16.8 | 17.1 | 35.84 | 14.98 | 33.29 |
| United States | 0.9 | 19.7 | 79.4 | 4.4 | 5.5 | 795 | 1.476 Trillion | 1.4 trillion |

| Country | Household Income | | Telephones | | Televisions | Radios |
|---|---|---|---|---|---|---|
| | Top 10% | Bottom 10% | Main lines | Cellular | | |
| Argentina | NA | NA | 7,500,000 | 1,800,000 | 7,950,000 | 24,003,000 |
| Bolivia | 31.7 | 2.3 | 368,874 | 7,229 | 900,000 | 5,025,000 |
| Brazil | 47.9 | 0.8 | 19,000,000 | 4,000,000 | 36,500,000 | 71,000,000 |
| Chile | 41.3 | 1.0 | 2,603,000 | 197,300 | 3,150,000 | 5,180,000 |
| Colombia | 44.0 | 1.0 | 5,433,565 | 1,800,229 | 4,590,000 | 21,000,000 |
| Costa Rica | 34.7 | 1.3 | 451,000 | 46,500 | 525,000 | 980,000 |
| Cuba | NA | NA | 353,000 | 1,939 | 2,640,000 | 3,900,000 |
| Dominican Republic | 39.6 | 1.6 | 569,000 | 33,000 | 770,000 | 1,440,000 |
| Ecuador | 37.6 | 2.3 | 748,000 | 49,776 | 1,550,000 | 4,150,000 |
| El Salvador | 38.3 | 1.2 | 380,000 | 13,475 | 600,000 | 2,750,000 |
| Guatemala | 46.6 | 0.6 | 342,000 | 29,999 | 640,000 | 835,000 |
| Honduras | 42.1 | 1.2 | 190,200 | 0 | 570,000 | 2,450,000 |
| Mexico | 36.6 | 1.8 | 9,600,000 | 2,020,000 | 25,600,000 | 31,000,000 |
| Nicaragua | 39.8 | 1.6 | 140,000 | 4,400 | 320,000 | 1,024,000 |
| Panama | 42.5 | 0.5 | 325,300 | 0 | 510,000 | 815,000 |
| Paraguay | 46.6 | 0.7 | 167,000 | 15,807 | 515,000 | 925,000 |
| Peru | 34.3 | 1.9 | 1,509,000 | 504,995 | 3,060,000 | 6,650,000 |
| Uruguay | NA | NA | 622,000 | 40,000 | 782,000 | 1,097,000 |
| Venezuela | 35.6 | 1.5 | 2,600,000 | 2,000,000 | 4,100,000 | 10,700,000 |
| United States | 28.5 | 1.5 | 178,000,000 | 55,212,000 | 219,000,000 | 575,000,000 |

Source: Data from *The World Factbook* 2005, Washington, D.C.: Central Intelligence Agency, 2000.
http://www.umsl.edu/services/govdocs/wofact2000/indexgeo.html

# Hugo Chavez Speaks at the 2005 World Social Forum

Ignacio Ramonet, in his introduction, mentioned that I am a new kind of leader. I accept this . . . but I am inspired by many old leaders.

Some very old like, for example Jesus Christ, one of the greatest revolutionaries, anti-imperialists fighters in the history of the world, the true Christ, the Redemptor of the Poor. Simón Bolívar, a guy that crisscrossed these lands, filling people with hope, and helping them become liberated.

Or that Argentine doctor, who crisscrossed our continent on a motorcycle, arriving in Central America to witness the gringo invasion of Guatemala.

Or that old guy with a beard, Fidel Castro, Abreu Lima, Artigas, San Martín, O'Higgins, Emiliano Zapata, Pancho Villa, Sandino, Morazán, Tupac Amaru.

Old guys that took up a commitment and now, from my heart, I understand them, because we have taken up a strong commitment. They have all returned.

Today we are millions.

Atahualpa has returned and he is millions, Tupac Amaru has returned and he is millions, Bolivar has returned and he is millions, Sucre, Zapata, and here we are, they have returned with us. In this filled up Gigantinho Stadium.

The World Social Forum, in these five years, has become a solid platform for debate, discussions, a solid, wide, varied, rich platform where the greater part of the excluded, those without a voice in the corridors of power, come here to express themselves and to raise their protests, here they come to sing, to say who they are, what they want, they come to recite their poems, their songs, their hope of finding consensus.

Today, at the WSF, no other space more appropriate, it is opportune to say that to save the world one of the first things we need is the conscience of the south.

It is possible that many in the north don't know this, but the future of the north depends on the south, because if we do not do what we must, if we truly do not make a better world real, if we fail, behind the marines' bayonets, behind the murderous bombs from Mr. Bush, if there is not enough strength, conscience, and organization in the south to resist the neo-imperialist attacks, if the Bush doctrine were to impose itself the world would be destroyed.

We resisted, we defended ourselves, and then went on the counteroffensive. As a result in 2003, for the first time, Venezuela recuperated its oil company, which had always been in the hands of the Venezuelan oligarchy and the North American Empire.

We were now directing almost 4 billion dollars to social investment, education, health, micro credits, housing, directed to the poorest. The neo-liberals say we are throwing money away but they were giving it away to the gringos, or shared it amongst themselves in their juicy business deals.

Before, education was privatized. That's the neo-liberal, imperialist plan, health systems were privatized, that cannot be, it's a fundamental human right. Health, education, water, energy, public services, that cannot be given to the voracity of private capital, that denies those rights to the people, that's the road to savagery, capitalism is savagery.

Every day I'm more convinced, less capitalism and more socialism.

167

We need to transcend capitalism, but capitalism cannot be transcended from within. Capitalism needs to be transcended via socialism, with equality and justice, that's the path to transcend the capitalist power.

I'm also convinced that it's possible to do it in democracy—but watch it, what type of democracy?—not the one Mr. Superman wants to impose.

Although I admire Che Guevara very much, his thesis was not viable. His guerrilla unit, perhaps 100 men in a mountain, that may have been valid in Cuba, but the conditions elsewhere were different, and that's why Che died in Bolivia, a Quixotic figure.

History showed that his thesis of one, two, three Vietnams did not work.

Today, the situation does not involve guerrilla cells, that can be surrounded by the Rangers or the Marines in a mountain, as they did to Che Guevara, they were only maybe 50 men against 500, now we are millions, how are they going to surround us? Careful, we might be the ones doing the surrounding . . . not yet, little by little.

This is not the same Latin America of even five years ago. I cannot, out of respect for you, comment on the internal situation of any other country. There in Venezuela, particularly the first two years, many of my partisans criticized me, asking me to go faster, that we had to be more radical. I did not consider it to be the right moment, because processes have stages. Compañeros, there are stages in the processes, there are rhythms that have to do with more than just the internal situation in every country, they have to do with the International situation. And even if some of you make noise, I will say it: I like Lula, I appreciate him, he is a good man, with a big heart, a brother, a compañero, and

I'm sure that Lula and the people of Brazil, with Nestor Kirchner and the Argentine people, with Tabarez Vazquez and the Uruguayan people, we will open the path towards the dream of a United Latin America, different, possible.

Source: ZNet, April 10, 2005,

http://www.Thirdworldtraveler.com/South_America/CapitalismSavagery_Chavez.html

I.

Because someone in the sixth century counted up

and called the inconceivable year when Christ

was born

Year One,

now the terror of the millennium,

the torments of the *fin-de-siecle* are ours.

Pity those who know

they are walking straight toward the abyss.

No doubt there is hope

for humanity.

For us, on the other hand,

there is only the certainty that tomorrow

we shall be condemned:

*–the stupid twentieth century,*

*its primitive, savage inhabitants–*

with the same fervor we used to banish

the *nineteenth-centurians*, authors,

with their ideas, their acts and inventions,

from the twentieth century, which only exists

in the imagination of those who watch

night gathering on this field of blood,

this planet of barbed wire fences, this

endless slaughterhouse that is dying

beneath the weight of all its victories.

II.

*A net full of holes* is our legacy to you,

passengers of the twenty-first century. The ship

is sinking for lack of air,

there are no more forests, the desert

shimmers in an ocean of greed.

We filled up the earth with trash,

poisoned the air, made

poverty triumphant on the planet.

Above all we killed.

Our century was

the century of death.

So much death,

so many dead in every country.

So much blood

spilled on this earth.

And everyone

said they were killing for the sake of tomorrow:

the quicksilver future, the hope

sifting like sand through our fingers.

In the name

of Good

Evil was imposed.

Doubtless there were other things.

171

It is up to you

to recognize them.

For now

the twentieth century has ended.

It encloses us

*like prehistoric amber traps the fly,*

says Milosz.

Let us plead, along with Neruda,

for *pity for this century.*

Because after all

this present created the future that is crashing

into the past.

The century lasted an instant

and ended in a second.

We say good-bye

and go to sleep in the amber prison.

Source: José Emilio Pacheco. *City of Memory and Other Poems.* Cynthia Steele and David Lauer, tran. San Francisco: City Lights Books, 1997), 31, 33, 35.